Bankruptcy Deadline Checklist

An Easy-to-Use Reference Guide for Case Management and Administration

Norman L. Pernick, Author

Jay A. Shulman, Editor

ABA Section of
BUSINESS LAW
Practical Resources for the Business

AMERICAN BAR ASSOCIATION
Defending Liberty
Pursuing Justice

© 2006 by the American Bar Association. All rights reserved.
Printed in the United States of America.

Cover designed by ABA Design.

Library of Congress Cataloging-in-Publication Data

Pernick, Norman L., 1959–
  Bankruptcy deadline checklist : an easy-to-use reference guide for case management and administration / Norman L. Pernick.— 3rd ed.
      p.   cm.
  Includes bibliographical references and index.
  ISBN-13: 978-1-59031-705-1 (alk. paper)
  ISBN-10: 1-59031-705-X (alk. paper)
  1. Bankruptcy—United States. I. Title.

KF1164.3.B36 2006
346.7307'8—dc22   2006007463

Discounts are available for books ordered in bulk. Custom covers are also available for bulk orders. Special consideration is given to state and local bars, CLE programs, and other bar-related organizations. Inquire at Book Publishing, American Bar Association, 321 North Clark Street, Chicago, Illinois 60610.

10 09 08 07 06 5 4 3 2 1

To
Paula,
Jessica, and
Sallie

ACKNOWLEDGMENTS

The author and editor wish to recognize the generous assistance of Renee L. Lowder and Jennifer Donaghy of Saul Ewing LLP, and G. David Dean, Esquire, also of Saul Ewing LLP, for his special contribution of time, energy, and expertise, beyond the call of duty in the preparation of this edition of the *Checklist*.

We also wish to recognize Kelly Conklin, formerly associate editor, THE BUSINESS LAWYER, University of Maryland School of Law, and Kate Stickles, Esquire, of Saul Ewing LLP, in the preparation of the prior editions of this book.

ACKNOWLEDGMENTS

CONTENTS

INTRODUCTION

I admit it. I wrote the first edition of *Bankruptcy Deadline Checklist* out of fear. After practicing bankruptcy law for several years, I was having trouble keeping track of all of the deadlines in the Chapter 7 (liquidation), Chapter 11 (reorganization), and Chapter 13 (adjustment of debts of an individual with regular income) bankruptcy cases that I was handling, and I was spending a lot of time trying to do so. I felt like a malpractice case waiting to happen. I needed an efficient way to locate and track all of the deadlines and filing requirements contained in the Bankruptcy Code and Bankruptcy Rules, and I was shocked to discover that there was no concise and easy-to-use published work that could grant me a restful night's sleep.

The original *Checklist* was a much simpler document. However, being the compulsive attorney that I am, the *Checklist* evolved over a period of several years into a compilation of all the time deadlines in the Bankruptcy Code and Rules that you see in this book. It has been updated periodically to incorporate relevant Code and Rule changes. The *Checklist* incorporates the recently enacted Bankruptcy Abuse Prevention and Consumer Protection Act of 2005, as well as the interim rules proposed to be adopted by the individual bankruptcy courts, and should also prove useful in learning the extensive changes contained in the most material revision of the Code since the 1978 enactment.

I am sure that you, too, will be genuinely surprised at all of the deadlines that you were unaware of, and I hope you will be pleased to add some order to your bankruptcy cases or study. If you believe as I do that tracking these deadlines is key, you can thank my wife for the book's publication; she urged me to undertake it based on the strong belief that others should be spared the task of creating one themselves and that their spouses should likewise be spared the involuntary job of suffering through that process.

The *Checklist* is obviously not a suspense novel meant to make me the next John Grisham. It is a very practical tool intended to be a quick reference guide to assist bankruptcy judges, attorneys, paralegals, credit managers, collection agents, professors, law students and others participating in bankruptcy cases or study. The *Checklist* is organized by chapter of the Bankruptcy Code (i.e., 1, 3, 5, 7, 11, 13, and 15), and, within each chapter, by Code section, with additional sections covering those items typically needed upon the filing of a case, rules on adversary proceedings, appeals, and notices. Due to the minimal number of Chapter 9 and 12 cases filed, deadlines under those Chapters are not included. The *Checklist* is meant to be a list of all of the potential deadlines in a case; it certainly is not necessary (and indeed would be unlikely) to use each deadline in a particular case.

To use the *Checklist,* simply look up the relevant Code section(s), which appear in numerical order and in the Index. Cross references for applicable Rules are provided. Code sections or Rules in bold designate the primary section or Rule containing the relevant deadline. Each deadline in the *Checklist* has a corresponding space for the insertion of a due date, so that the user may calculate and maintain a master list of deadlines in each case if that is desired.

The *Checklist* has been printed in an easily transportable size for ease of use at your desk, in court, at seminars, in client meetings, and so forth.

Norm Pernick

BANKRUPTCY DEADLINE CHECKLIST[1]

Filing of Case[2]

DUE DATE	ACTION	CODE §	RULE[3]	EXPLANATION; TIME TO ACT
	Retainer letter and retainer			Recommended at inception of representation.
	Notice of appearance and request for notices		2002[4] 9010(b)	Recommended at beginning of case; however, filing of a notice of appearance may result in submission to jurisdiction of bankruptcy court.
	Venue of cases under Bankruptcy Code	28 USC § 1408		Case may be commenced in district in which domicile, residence, principal place of business in U.S., or principal assets in U.S. have been located for 180 days immediately preceding commencement of case, or for longer portion of 180 day period than domicile, residence, principal place of business in U.S., or principal assets in U.S. were located in any other district. Cases may also be commenced in a district where there is a pending case of an affiliate, general partner or partnership of the debtor.

[1] This checklist is applicable to cases under Chapters 7 (liquidation), 11 (reorganization), and 13 (individual with regular income) of the Bankruptcy Code and Rules, as amended through October 17, 2005, the general effective date of the Bankruptcy Abuse Prevention and Consumer Protection Act ("BAPCPA"), Pub. L. No. 109-8, 199 Stat. 23, enacted on April 20, 2005. All bankruptcy cases are filed under Chapters 7, 9, 11, 12, or 13 and now under Chapter 15 as foreign main proceedings or foreign nonmain proceedings. This checklist does not cover Chapters 9 and 12 and only includes a brief checklist for Chapter 15. Many general provisions, however, apply no matter which chapter a case is filed under, and they must also be consulted (e.g., Chapters 1, 3 , and 5, and the rules cited herein). This checklist also assumes that cases were filed on or after October 17, 2005, the general effective date. Unless made applicable to cases filed prior to that date by BAPCPA, the events and deadlines applicable to cases filed prior to October 15, 2005 may be materially different, in accordance with prior law.

[2] This Section ("Filing of Case") is meant as a general quick reference tool highlighting some of the typical documents and deadlines to be filed and followed at the beginning of a case. It is meant to be illustrative and not exhaustive.

[3] The effective date of BAPCPA left insufficient time for the promulgation of amendments to the Federal Rules of Bankruptcy Procedure ("Rules") in accordance with the Rules Enabling Act, 28 U.S.C. §§ 2071–77. The proposed "permanent" national rules implementing the changes to the Bankruptcy Code are anticipated to be published by the Advisory Committee on Bankruptcy Rules (the "Advisory Committee") of the Standing Committee on Rules and Practices of the Judicial Conference of the United States (the "Standing Committee") by August, 2006, so that the Rules can be commented upon, completed, approved by the Supreme Court and not acted upon by Congress, and would be come effective by about December, 2008. To make available rules that may be used until such date, the Advisory Committee has prepared Interim Rules, approved by the Standing Committee, which were published in August 2005. Some modifications to the Interim Rules were proposed on October 13, 2005. The Advisory Committee and Standing Committee have recommended and urge all bankruptcy courts to adopt such Interim Rules as local rules, since a procedure is not available for the implementation of interim rules on a national basis. This checklist has incorporated the Interim Rules and identified such Interim Rules when they are applicable to the procedure. However, counsel are specifically cautioned (in addition to the general caution contained in footnote 4, below), to ascertain whether the Interim Rules have been adopted by a local bankruptcy court and whether they have been amended by such court.

[4] This checklist is intended to be a quick reference guide only; the relevant Code sections and rules and experienced counsel should always be consulted to ensure complete compliance, including effective dates of recent amendments and possible amendments adopted after the date of publication of this checklist. Code sections or rules in bold designate the primary section or rule containing the relevant deadline.

DUE DATE	ACTION	CODE §	RULE	EXPLANATION; TIME TO ACT
	Venue of cases ancillary to foreign proceeding			A case under Chapter 15 of the Bankruptcy Code may be commenced in the district court of the United States for the district: (1) in which the debtor has its principal place of business or principal assets in the United States; (2) if the debtor does not have a place of business or assets in the United States, in which there is pending against the debtor an action or proceeding in a Federal or State court; (3) in any other case, in which venue will be consistent with the interests of justice and convenience of the parties, having regard to the relief sought by the foreign representative.
	Change of venue for cases	28 USC § 1412	1014(a) (1)	If a petition is filed in a proper district, on timely motion of a party in interest, and after hearing on notice to the petitioners, the U.S. Trustee, and other entities as directed by the court, the case may be transferred to any other district if the court determines that the transfer is in the interest of justice or for the convenience of the parties.
	Dismissal or change of venue for case filed in wrong district	28 USC § 1406	1014(a) (2)	The right to dismissal of a case filed in the wrong venue is authorized in 28 USC § 1406, the general federal statute on cases filed in an incorrect venue. This statute authorizes dismissal or, if it is in the interest of justice, transfer of venue to a district in which the case could properly be filed. Rule 1014(2) is based on the assumption that dismissal is an available option and permits dismissal or transfer on motion of a party in interest, and after a hearing on notice to the petitioners, the U.S. Trustee, and other entities as directed by the court.
	Credit counseling requirement for individual debtor	109(h)(1)		Subject to 109(h)(2), (3) and (4), an individual may not be a debtor unless the individual has, during 180 days preceding the petition date, received from an approved nonprofit budget and credit counseling agency described in § 111(a) an individual or group briefing (including a brief by telephone or Internet) that outlined the opportunities for available credit counseling and assisted such individual in performing a related budget analysis. See Chapter 1: General Provisions for exceptions.
	Declaration by bankruptcy petition preparer (as defined by § 110(a)(1) of fees paid by and charged to the debtor)	110(h)(2)		Must be filed under penalty of perjury with the petition. See Chapter 1: General Provisions for details.

DUE DATE	ACTION	CODE §	RULE	EXPLANATION; TIME TO ACT
	Filing of petition in voluntary and involuntary cases; contents of petition	**301** **302** **303(b)**	**1002(a)** **1003**	Case begins when a petition is filed with bankruptcy court. See Chapter 3: Case Administration for details.
	Payment of filing fee	**28 USC § 1930**	**1006**	Ordinarily paid at the time the petition is filed. See Chapter 3: Case Administration for details and exceptions for installment payment and waiver of filing fee.
	Service of involuntary petition and summons	303(b)	**1010** 704	On filing of involuntary petition or petition commencing a case ancillary to foreign proceeding, clerk shall forthwith issue a summons. See Chapter 3: Case Administration for details.
	List of creditors and other parties in voluntary case	301 **521**	**1007(a)** **(1)**	Debtor must file with petition a list containing the names and addresses of each entity included or to be included on Schedules D, E, F, G and H. See Chapter 3: Case Administration for details.
	List of creditors and other parties in involuntary case	303 **521**	**1007(a)** **(2)**	Debtor must file within 15 days after entry of order for relief a list containing name and address of each entity included or to be included on Schedules D, E, F, G and H. See Chapter 3: Case Administration for details.
	List of equity security holders in Chapter 11 case	521	**1007(a)** **(3)**	Debtor shall file within 15 days after entry of order of relief a list of debtor's equity security holders of each class showing the number and kind of interests registered in the name of each holder, and the last known address or place of business of each holder.
	Disclosure of list of security holders by party other than debtor		**1007(k)**	After notice and hearing, court may direct an entity other than debtor or trustee to disclose any list of security holders of debtor in its possession or under its control.
	Extension of time for filing lists required by § 1007(a)		**1007(a)** **(5)**	May be granted only after motion for cause is shown and after notice to U.S. Trustee and any trustee or committee appointed.
	Attorney disclosure of compensation paid or promised to attorney for debtor within one year prior to petition date	329(a)	**2016(b)**	Within 15 days after order for relief, attorney must file and transmit § 329 statement to U.S. Trustee; supplemental statement must be filed and transmitted to U.S. Trustee within 15 days after any payment or agreement not previously disclosed. See Chapter 3: Case Administration for details.

DUE DATE	ACTION	CODE §	RULE	EXPLANATION; TIME TO ACT
	Appointment of professional persons	327	2014	Beginning of case and with court approval. See Chapter 3: Case Administration for details.
	Notice of order for relief to parties in interest, including holder of community claim (as appropriate)	342(a)	2002(d), (f)	Within reasonable time and as directed by court. See Chapter 3: Case Administration for details.
	Proper identification of debtor	342(c)		Notices required to be given to creditors must contain the name, address, and last 4 digits of the taxpayer identification number of the debtor.
	Evidence that debtor is debtor in possession		2011(a)	Clerk may so certify whenever evidence is required that debtor is debtor in possession.
	Notice to individual debtors whose debts are primarily consumer debts	342(b)		Before the commencement of the case, the clerk shall give such individual written notice containing a brief description of Chapters 7, 11, 12 and 13 and the other information specified in § 342(c). See Chapter 3: Case Administration for details.
	Duty of debtor to file Schedule of Assets and Liabilities, Executory Contracts, Schedule of Income and Expenditures, and Statement of Affairs and other documents in voluntary case	521(a)(1) 521(c)	1007(a), Interim 1007(b)(b) and Interim 1007(c)	See Chapter 3: Case Administration for details.
	Filing of statements and schedules when Chapter 11 or Chapter 13 case has been converted or reconverted to Chapter 7 case		1019(1) (A)	Lists, inventories, schedules, and statements of financial affairs previously filed are deemed filed in Chapter 7 case unless court directs otherwise; if not previously filed, debtor must comply with Rule 1007 as if order for relief had been entered on an involuntary petition on the date of entry of order directing that case continue under Chapter 7.
	List of 20 largest creditors in a voluntary Chapter 11 case		1007(d)	With the petition. See Chapter 3: Case Administration for details.
	General right to amend voluntary petitions, lists, schedules, and statements		1009(a)	May be amended by debtor as a matter of course at any time before the case is closed; debtor must give notice of the amendment to the trustee and to any entity affected thereby.

Chapter 1, General Provisions, generally applies to cases filed under Chapters 7, 11, 12, 13, and (in part) Chapter 15 of the Code. Chapter 1 contains a lengthy set of definitions that should always be consulted when reviewing other sections of the Code, as well as sections dealing with rules of construction, power of the court, sovereign immunity, statutes of limitation, and rules for who may be a debtor under a particular Chapter.

Chapter 1: General Provisions

DUE DATE	ACTION	CODE §	RULE	EXPLANATION; TIME TO ACT
	Creditor	101(10)(A)		An entity that has a claim against the debtor that arose at the time of or before the order for relief, concerning the debtor.
	Disinterested person	101(14)		A person who • Is not a creditor, an equity security holder, or an insider; • Is not and was not, within 2 years before the date of filing, a director, officer, employee, etc., of debtor; and • Does not have an interest materially adverse to the interest of the estate, any class of creditors, or equity security holders.
	Domestic support obligation	101(14A)		A debt that accrues before, on, or after the date of the order for relief, including interest that accrues on that debt as provided under applicable nonbankruptcy law that is: • owed to or recoverable by a spouse, former spouse, or child of the debtor or such or child's parent, legal guardian, or responsible relative or a governmental unit; • in the nature of alimony, maintenance, or support (including assistance provided by a governmental unit) of such spouse, former spouse, or child of the debtor or such child's parent, without regard to whether such debt is expressly so designated; • established or subject to establishment before, on, or after the date of the order for relief, by reason of applicable provisions of a separation agreement, divorce decree, or property settlement agreement, an order of a court of record, or a determination made in accordance with applicable nonbankruptcy law by a governmental unit; or • not assigned to a nongovernmental entity, unless that obligation is assigned voluntarily by the spouse, former spouse, child of the debtor, or such child's parent, legal guardian, or responsible relative for the purpose of collecting the debt.

DUE DATE	ACTION	CODE §	RULE	EXPLANATION; TIME TO ACT
	Health care business	101(27A)		Any public or private entity (without regard to whether that entity is organized for profit or not for profit) that is primarily engaged in offering to the general public facilities and services for: (1) the diagnosis or treatment of injury, deformity, or disease; and (2) surgical, drug treatment, psychiatric, or obstetric care.
				A health care business includes any: • general or specialized hospital; • ancillary ambulatory, emergency, or surgical treatment facility; • hospice; • home health agency; and • other health care institution that is similar.
				A health care business includes any long-term care facility, including any: • skilled nursing facility; • intermediate care facility; • assisted living facility; • home for the aged; • domiciliary care facility; and • health care institution that is related to a facility referred to above if such institution is primarily engaged in offering room, board, laundry, or personal assistance with activities of daily living and incidentals to activities of daily living.
	Repo participant	101(46)		An entity that, any time before the filing of the petition, has an outstanding repurchase agreement with the debtor.
	Small business debtor	101(51D)		A person engaged in commercial or business activities (including any affiliate of such person that is also a debtor under this title and excluding a person whose primary activity is the business of owning or operating real property or activities incidental thereto) that has aggregate noncontingent, liquidated secured and unsecured debts as of the date of the petition or the order for relief in an amount not more than $3,000,000 (excluding debts owed to 1 or more affiliates or insiders) for a case in which the U.S. Trustee has not appointed under § 1102(a)(1) a committee of unsecured creditors or where the court has determined that the committee of unsecured creditors is not sufficiently active and representative to provide effective oversight of the debtor; but does not include any member of a group of affiliated debtors that has aggregate noncontingent liquidated secured and unsecured debts in an amount greater than $3,000,000 (excluding debt owed to 1 or more affiliates or insiders).

DUE DATE	ACTION	CODE §	RULE	EXPLANATION; TIME TO ACT
	Definition of "after notice and a hearing" or similar phrase	102(1)(A)		"After notice and a hearing" or similar phrase means after such notice as is appropriate in the particular circumstances, and such opportunity for hearing as is appropriate in the particular circumstances.
		102(1)(B)		However, such phrase in the statute or rules authorizes an act without a hearing if notice was given properly and if hearing is not requested timely by party in interest, or there is insufficient time for a hearing to be commenced before act must be done, and court authorizes the act.
	Ability of court to manage case	105(d)		Court, on its own motion or on request of a party in interest, shall hold a status conference as is necessary to further the expeditious and economical resolution of the case, and may issue an order at that status conference prescribing such limitations and conditions as court deems appropriate to ensure that the case is handled expeditiously and economically, including an order that: (1) sets date by which trustee must assume or reject an executory contract or unexpired lease; or (2) in a Chapter 11 case, enters order that: • sets date by which debtor or trustee shall file disclosure statement and plan; • sets date by which debtor or trustee shall solicit acceptances of a plan; • sets date by which a party in interest other than debtor may file a plan; • sets date by which a proponent of a plan, other than the debtor, shall solicit acceptances of plan; • fixes scope and format of notice to be provided regarding disclosure statement hearing are fixed; or combines hearing on disclosure statement and confirmation.
	Extension of time for debtor to commence action	108(a)		If the period within which debtor may commence action has not expired before petition date, later of the period set by nonbankruptcy law, the court order, or agreement (including any suspension of such period occurring on or after commencement of case), or 2 years from order for relief.

DUE DATE	ACTION	CODE §	RULE	EXPLANATION; TIME TO ACT
	Extension of time	**108(b)**		Except as provided in § 108(a), if applicable nonbankruptcy law, an order entered in a nonbankruptcy proceeding, or an agreement fixes a period within which the debtor or an individual protected under § 1301 may file any pleading, demand, notice, or proof of claim or loss, cure a default, or perform any other similar act, and such period has not expired before the date of the filing of the petition, the trustee may only file, cure, or perform, as the case may be, before the later of: (1) the end of such period, including any suspension of such period occurring on or after the commencement of the case; or (2) 60 days after the order for relief.
	Extension of time to commence an action which commencement is stayed	**108(c)**		Except as provided in § 524 (discharge of debts), if applicable nonbankruptcy law, an order entered in a nonbankruptcy proceeding, or an agreement fixes a period for commencing or continuing a civil action in a court other than a bankruptcy court on a claim against the debtor, or against an individual with respect to which such individual is protected under § 1201 or § 1301, and such period has not expired before the date of the filing of the petition, then such period does not expire until the later of (1) the end of such period, including any suspension of such period occurring on or after the commencement of the case; or (2) 30 days after notice of the termination or expiration of the stay.
	Eligibility for Chapter 13	**109(e)** 104(b)		Only an individual with regular income that owes, on the date of the filing of the petition, noncontingent, liquidated, unsecured debts of less than $307,675 and noncontingent, liquidated, secured debts of less than $922,975, or an individual with regular income and such individual's spouse, except a stockbroker or a commodity broker, that owe, on the date of the filing of the petition, noncontingent, liquidated, unsecured debts that aggregate less than $307,675 and noncontingent, liquidated, secured debts of less than $922,975 may be a debtor under Chapter 13. Dollar amounts are subject to adjustment under § 104(b). The foregoing dollar amounts apply to cases commenced on or after April 1, 2004.

DUE DATE	ACTION	CODE §	RULE	EXPLANATION; TIME TO ACT
	Prohibition on individual becoming debtor a second time	109(g)		No individual may be a debtor under Title 11 who has been a debtor in a case pending under Title 11 at any time in the preceding 180 days if: (1) the case was dismissed by the court for willful failure of debtor to abide by orders of the court, or to appear before the court in proper prosecution of the case; or (2) debtor requested and obtained the voluntary dismissal of the case following the filing of a request for relief from the automatic stay.
	Credit counseling requirement for individual Chapter 7	109(h)(1)		Subject to §§ 109(h)(2) and (3), an individual may not be a debtor unless the individual has, during 180 days preceding the petition date, received from an approved nonprofit budget and credit counseling agency described in § 111(a), an individual or group briefing (including a brief by telephone or Internet) that outlines the opportunities for available credit counseling and assisted such individual in performing a related budget analysis.
	Credit counseling requirement for filing Chapter 7 by individual not applicable in districts where credit counseling agencies not able to provide adequate services	109(h)(2)		The credit counseling requirement of §109(h)(1) shall not apply with respect to a debtor who resides in a district for which the U.S. Trustee (or the bankruptcy administrator, if any) determines that the approved nonprofit budget and credit counseling agencies for such district are not reasonably able to provide adequate services to the additional individuals who would otherwise seek credit counseling from such agencies.
	Limited exigent circumstances exemption to credit counseling requirement	109(h)(3)		The credit counseling requirement shall not apply to a debtor who submits a certificate to the court that: (1) describes exigent circumstances that merit a waiver of the requirement; (2) states that the debtor requested credit counseling, but was unable to obtain such counseling during the 5-day period beginning on the date the debtor made the request; and (3) is satisfactory with the court. The exemption described above shall cease to apply on the date the debtor meets the credit counseling requirement, but in no case may the exemption apply to that debtor after the 30th day after the petition date, except that the court, for cause, may extend the exemption for an additional 15 days.

DUE DATE	ACTION	CODE §	RULE	EXPLANATION; TIME TO ACT
	Notice to the debtor by bankruptcy petition preparer	**110(b)(2)** **110(c)**		Before preparing any document for filing or accepting any fees from a debtor, the bankruptcy petition preparer shall provide to the debtor a written notice on the Official Form which shall inform the debtor in simple language that a bankruptcy petition preparer is not an attorney and may not practice law or give legal advice. The notice shall: (1) be signed by the debtor and, under penalty of perjury, by the bankruptcy petition preparer; and (2) be filed with any document prepared by the bankruptcy petition preparer.
	Requirements of bankruptcy petition preparer to sign documents and provide identifying number	**110(b)(1)** **110(c)**		A bankruptcy petition preparer who prepares a document for filing shall sign the document and print on the document the preparer's name and address. If a bankruptcy petition preparer is not an individual, then an officer, principal, responsible person, or partner of the bankruptcy petition preparer shall be required to sign the document for filing; and print on the document the name and address of that officer, principal, responsible person, or partner. A bankruptcy petition preparer who prepares a document for filing shall place on the document, after the preparer's signature, an identifying number that identifies individuals who prepared the document in accordance with § 110(c)(2).
	Requirements of bankruptcy petition preparer to provide copies of prepared document to debtor	**110(d)**		A bankruptcy petition preparer shall, not later than the time at which a document for filing is presented for the debtor's signature, furnish to the debtor a copy of the document.
				For requirements of declaration of fees of the bankruptcy petition preparer to be made with the petition, *see* Chapter 3, Case Administration.

Chapter 3, Case Administration, generally applies to cases filed under Chapters 7, 11, 12, 13, and (in part) Chapter 15 of the Code. The topics generally include the commencement of a case, officers, case administration and administrative powers. Specific subjects covered include voluntary and involuntary cases, abstention, debtor reporting requirements, compensation of trustees, officers and professional persons, and ombudsmen in consumer cases. Chapter 3 also contains the rules for creditor meetings, examinations of the debtor, state and local taxes, conversion and dismissal. Adequate protection, the automatic stay, the use, sale or lease of property, obtaining credit, executory contracts, and unexpired leases and utility service are also dealt with.

Chapter 3: Case Administration

DUE DATE	ACTION	CODE §	RULE	EXPLANATION; TIME TO ACT
	Commencement of voluntary case	301 302	1002(a)	Voluntary case is commenced by filing of petition by entity that may be debtor under chosen chapter; commencement of voluntary case under § 301 constitutes order for relief.
	Filing list of creditors and other parties in a voluntary case	301 302 521(a)(1)	1007(a)	In a voluntary case, the debtor shall file with the petition a list containing the name and address of each entity included or to be included on Schedules D, E, F, G and H.
	Declaration of fees received from the debtor by bankruptcy petition preparer	301 110(h)(2)	2016(c)[1]	A declaration under penalty of perjury by the bankruptcy petition preparer shall be filed together with the petition, disclosing any fee received from or on behalf of the debtor within 12 months immediately prior to the filing of the case, and any unpaid fee charged to the debtor.
	Filing of corporate ownership statement in a voluntary case	301 521(a)(1)	1007(a) 7007.1	If the debtor is a corporation, other than a governmental unit, the debtor shall file with the petition a corporate ownership statement containing the information described in Rule 7007.1.
	List of equity security holders in Chapter 11 case	301 521(a)(1)	1007(a)(3)	In a Chapter 11 reorganization case, unless the court orders otherwise, the debtor shall file within 15 days after entry of the order for relief a list of the debtor's equity security holders of each class showing the number and kind of interests registered in the name of each holder, and the last known address or place of business of each holder.
	Extension of time to file lists required by Rule 1007(a)		1007(a)(4)	Any extension of time for the filing of the lists required by this subdivision may be granted only on motion for cause shown and on notice to the U.S. Trustee and to any trustee, any committee elected pursuant to § 705 or appointed pursuant to § 1102, or other party as the court may direct.

[1] The current version of Rule 2016(c) reflects the § 110(h) prior to BAPCPA and is inconsistent with the revised statute and the Interim Rules have not yet addressed the changes. Prior to BAPCPA, the bankruptcy petition preparer could file the declaration within 10 days of the filing of the petition.

DUE DATE	ACTION	CODE §	RULE	EXPLANATION; TIME TO ACT
	List of 20 largest creditors in a voluntary Chapter 11 case		1007(d)	A debtor in a voluntary Chapter 11 reorganization case shall file with the petition a list containing the name, address and claim of the creditors that hold the 20 largest unsecured claims, excluding insiders, as prescribed by the appropriate Official Form.
	Disclosure of list of security holders by party other than the debtor		1007(i)	After notice and a hearing for cause shown, the court may direct an entity other than the debtor or trustee to disclose any list of security holders of the debtor in its possession or under its control, indicating the name, address and security held by any of them.
	Payment of filing fee	28 USC § 1930(a)	Interim 1006(a)	Every petition shall be accompanied by the filing fee except as provided in 28 USC § 1930(a)(7) (payment in installments by individual) or 28 USC § 1930(a) (payment in installments).
	Application by individual for permission to pay filing fee in installments	28 USC § 1930(a)(7)	Interim 1006(b)	A voluntary petition by an individual shall be accepted for filing if accompanied by the debtor's signed application, prepared as prescribed by the appropriate Official Form, stating that the debtor is unable to pay the filing fee except in installments. If the court grants leave to pay the filing fee in installments, all installments must be paid in full before the debtor or Chapter 13 trustee may make further payments to an attorney or any other person who renders service to the debtor in connection with the case.
	Request for waiver of filing fee	28 USC § 1930(f)	Interim 1006(c)	A voluntary petition filed by an individual shall be accepted for filing if accompanied by the debtor's application requesting a waiver under 28 USC § 1930(f), prepared as prescribed by the appropriate Official Form. The bankruptcy court or district court may waive the fee if such individual has income less than 150% of the income official poverty line and cannot pay the fee in installments.

DUE DATE	ACTION	CODE §	RULE	EXPLANATION; TIME TO ACT
	Designation of small business debtor in voluntary Chapter 11 petition		**Interim 1020(a)**	In a voluntary Chapter 11 case, the debtor shall state in the petition whether the debtor is a small business debtor. Except as provided in Interim Rule 1020(c), the status of the case with respect to whether it is a small business case shall be in accordance with the debtor's statement, unless and until the court enters an order finding that the debtor's statement is incorrect.
	Designation of health care business debtor in voluntary or involuntary Chapter 7 or 11 petition or in voluntary Chapter 9 petition	**301 303**	**Interim 1021**	Unless the court orders otherwise, if a petition in a case under Chapter 7, Chapter 9, or Chapter 11 states that the debtor is a health care business, the case shall proceed as a case in which the debtor is a health care business. The U.S. Trustee or a party in interest may file a motion for a determination as to whether the debtor is a health care business. The motion shall be transmitted to the U.S. Trustee and served on the debtor, the trustee, any committee elected under § 705 or appointed under § 1102 or its authorized agent, or, if the case is a Chapter 9 municipality case or a Chapter 11 reorganization case in which no committee of unsecured creditors has been appointed, on the creditors included on the list filed under Rule 1007(d), and such other entities as the court may direct.
	Objection to designation as a small business case		**Interim 1020(b) and (d)**	Except as provided in Interim Rule 1020(c), the U.S. Trustee or a party in interest may file an objection to the debtor's designation as a small business debtor not later than 30 days after the conclusion of the meeting of creditors held under § 341(a), or within 30 days after any amendment to the designation, whichever is later. Any objection or request for a determination under this rule shall be governed by Rule 9014 and served on the debtor, the debtor's attorney, the U.S. Trustee, the trustee, any committee appointed under § 1102 or its authorized agent, or, if no committee of unsecured creditors has been appointed, on the creditors included on the list filed under Rule 1007(d), and on such other entities as the court may direct.

DUE DATE	ACTION	CODE §	RULE	EXPLANATION; TIME TO ACT
			Interim 1020(c)	In accordance with § 101(51D), if the U.S. Trustee has appointed a committee of unsecured creditors under § 1102(a)(1), the case shall proceed as a small business case only if, and from the time when, the court enters an order determining that the committee has not been sufficiently active and representative to provide effective oversight of the debtor and that the debtor satisfies all the other requirements for being a small business. A request for such determination may be filed by the U.S. Trustee or a party in interest only within a reasonable time after the failure of the committee to be sufficiently active and representative. The debtor may file a request for a determination at any time as to whether the committee has been sufficiently active and representative.
	Commencement of a involuntary case	**303(a) and (b)**	**1003**	An involuntary case is commenced by the filing of an involuntary petition: (1) by three or more entities, each of which is either a holder of a claim against such person that is not contingent as to liability or the subject of a bona fide dispute as to liability or amount, or an indenture trustee representing such a holder, if such noncontingent, undisputed claims aggregate at least $12,300 more than the value of any lien on property of the debtor securing such claims held by the holders of such claims; or (2) if there are fewer than 12 such holders, excluding any employee or insider of such person and any transferee of a transfer that is voidable under §§ 544, 545, 547, 548, 549, or 724(a), by one or more of such holders that hold in the aggregate at least $12,300 of such claims.
	Involuntary petition against a partnership	**303(b)(3)**	**1004**	Petitioning partners or other petitioners must promptly serve a copy of the petition upon each general partner who is not a petitioner. A summons is promptly issued by the clerk for each general partner who is not a petitioner for service in accordance with Rule 1010.
	Service of an involuntary petition		**1010 7004(a) and (b)**	Clerk promptly issues a summons for service, which is served, along with a copy of the petition, on debtor in accordance with Rule 7004(a) or (b).

DUE DATE	ACTION	CODE §	RULE	EXPLANATION; TIME TO ACT
	Joining creditors in involuntary case	303(c)	1003(b)	After filing, but before case is dismissed or relief is ordered, additional noncontingent unsecured creditor may join in petition.
	Contesting an involuntary petition	303(d)	1011(a)	The debtor, or a general partner of a partnership debtor who did not join in the petition or a person is who is alleged to be a general partner but denies the allegation, may file an answer to the petition.
	Requirement of petitioners in involuntary case to file bond	303(e)		After notice and hearing, the court may require the petitioners to file a bond to indemnify the debtor for such amounts as the court may later allow under § 303(i).
	Time to file answer to the involuntary petition	303(d)	1011(b) 1011(c) 1018 7001	The debtor, or a general partner of a partnership debtor that did not join the petition may answer within 20 days after service of summons; service of a motion under FRCP. 12(b) shall extend the time for filing and serving a responsive pleading as permitted by FRCP. 12(a); contested involuntary petitions are governed by certain adversary proceeding rules.
	Documents to be filed by debtor with answer in involuntary case		1003(b)	If answer to involuntary petition filed by fewer than 3 creditors avers the existence of 12 or more creditors, debtor shall file with the answer a list of all creditors with their addresses, a brief statement of the nature of their claims and the amounts of their claims.
	Order for relief in involuntary case	303(h)	1013(a) 1013(b) 1011(b) 1018 7001	Court must determine issues of contested involuntary petition at the earliest practicable time and forthwith enter an order for relief, dismiss the petition, or enter other appropriate orders. If no pleading or other defense to a petition is filed within 20 days after service of summons, the court shall enter order for relief on the next day, or as soon thereafter as practicable.
	List of 20 largest creditors in a involuntary Chapter 11 case	303(h) 521	1007(d)	In an involuntary Chapter 11 reorganization case, a list containing the name, address and claim of the creditors that hold the 20 largest unsecured claims, excluding insiders, as prescribed by the appropriate Official Form, shall be filed by the debtor within 2 days after entry of the order for relief under § 303(h).
	Filing list of creditors in an involuntary case	303(h) 521	1007(a)(2)	In an involuntary case, the debtor shall file within 15 days after entry of the order for relief, a list containing the name and address of each creditor unless a schedule of liabilities has been filed.

DUE DATE	ACTION	CODE §	RULE	EXPLANATION; TIME TO ACT
	Designation of small business debtor in voluntary Chapter 11 petition		Interim 1020(a)	In an involuntary Chapter 11 case, the debtor shall file within 15 days after entry of the order for relief a statement as to whether the debtor is a small business debtor. Except as provided in Interim Rule 1020(c), the status of the case with respect to whether it is a small business case shall be in accordance with the debtor's statement, unless and until the court enters an order finding that the debtor's statement is incorrect.
	Continuation of business of debtor in involuntary case in "gap" period	303(f)		Notwithstanding § 363, except to extent court orders otherwise, and until order for relief is entered in case, any business of debtor may continue to operate, and debtor may continue to use, acquire, or dispose of property as if an involuntary case had not been commenced.
	Dismissal of involuntary petition	303(j)	1017(c)	Only after notice to all creditors and a hearing may the court dismiss an involuntary petition: (1) on the motion of a petitioner; (2) on consent of all petitioners and the debtor; or (3) for want of prosecution.
	Dismissal or abstention	305	1017(d)	After notice and hearing.
	Small business debtor reporting requirements	308		Section 308 deals with periodic financial and other reports to be filed by the small business debtor, but § 308 will not take effect until 60 days after the permanent rules and forms to implement § 308 are promulgated pursuant to 28 USC § 2075.
	Deadline for trustee to file trustee bond	322(a)	2010	Within 5 days after selection and before beginning official duties.
	Proceeding on trustee's bond	322(d)	2010 7001 9025	Before expiration of 2 years after the date on which trustee was discharged.
	Removal of trustee or examiner	324(a)	2012(b)	The court, after notice and a hearing, may remove a trustee, other than the U.S. Trustee, or an examiner, for cause. When a trustee dies, resigns, is removed, or otherwise ceases to hold office during the pendency of a case under the Code: (1) the successor is automatically substituted as a party in any pending action, proceeding, or matter; and (2) the successor trustee shall prepare, file, and transmit to the U.S. Trustee an accounting of the prior administration of the estate.

DUE DATE	ACTION	CODE §	RULE	EXPLANATION; TIME TO ACT
	Employment of professional persons	327	2014	The trustee, with the court's approval, may employ one or more attorneys, accountants, appraisers, auctioneers, or other professional persons, that do not hold or represent an interest adverse to the estate, and that are disinterested persons, to represent or assist the trustee in carrying out the trustee's duties. An order approving the employment of attorneys, accountants, appraisers, auctioneers, agents, or other professionals pursuant to § 327, § 1103, or § 1114 shall be made only on application of the trustee or committee.
	Employment by trustee of special counsel	327(e)	2014	The trustee, with the court's approval, may employ, for a specified special purpose, other than to represent the trustee in conducting the case, an attorney that has represented the debtor, if in the best interest of the estate, and if such attorney does not represent or hold any interest adverse to the debtor or to the estate with respect to the matter on which such attorney is to be employed. Such employment is made by application in the same manner as for professionals under § 327(a).
	Disclosure of compensation	329(a)	2016(b)	Any attorney representing a debtor in the case, or in connection with such a case, whether or not such attorney applies for compensation under the Code, shall file with the court a statement of the compensation paid or agreed to be paid within 15 days after the order for relief, if such payment or agreement was made after one year before the date of the filing of the petition, for services rendered or to be rendered in contemplation of or in connection with the case by such attorney, and the source of such compensation. A supplemental statement shall be filed and transmitted to the U.S. Trustee within 15 days after any payment or agreement not previously disclosed.
	Compensation of professional persons	330	2016(a)	After notice to the parties in interest and the U.S. Trustee and a hearing, the court may award to a trustee, a consumer privacy ombudsman, an examiner, a patient care ombudsman, or a professional person employed under §§ 327 or 1103 reasonable compensation for actual, necessary services rendered and reimbursement for actual, necessary expenses. The entity seeking compensation shall file an application in accordance with Rule 2016(a).

DUE DATE	ACTION	CODE §	RULE	EXPLANATION; TIME TO ACT
	Interim fee application for compensation and reimbursement of expenses	**331** 328 330(a) 503(b)	**2016(a)**	A trustee, examiner, debtor's attorney or other professional person may apply to the court for an award of interim compensation not more than once every 120 days from order for relief, unless the court permits more frequent applications in accordance with Rule 2016(a).
	Appointment of consumer privacy ombudsman	**332(a)** **363(b)(1)(B)**	**Interim** **6004(g)**	If a hearing is required under § 363(b)(1)(B) for the sale or lease of personally identifiable information about individuals, the court shall order the U.S. Trustee to appoint, not later than 5 days before the commencement of the hearing, one disinterested person (other than the U.S. Trustee) to serve as the consumer privacy ombudsman in the case and shall require that notice of such hearing be timely given to such ombudsman. A motion for authority to sell or lease personally identifiable information under § 363(b)(1)(B) shall include a request for an order directing the U.S. Trustee to appoint the ombudsman. The motion shall be served on any committee elected under § 705 or appointed under § 1102, or in a Chapter 11 case in which no committee of unsecured creditors has been appointed, on the creditors included on the list of creditors filed under Rule 1007(d), and on such other entities as the court may direct. The motion shall be transmitted to the U.S. Trustee. If the ombudsman is appointed under § 332, no later than 5 days before the hearing on the motion under § 363(b)(1)(B), the U.S. Trustee shall file a report certifying the appointment, including the name and address of the person appointed. The U.S. Trustee's report shall be accompanied by a verified statement of the person appointed setting forth the person's connections with the debtor, creditors, any other party in interest, their respective attorneys and accountants, the U.S. Trustee, or any person employed in the office of the U.S. Trustee.

DUE DATE	ACTION	CODE §	RULE	EXPLANATION; TIME TO ACT
	Appointment of patient care ombudsman	333(a) and (b)	**Interim 2007.2(a), (b), and (c)**	If the debtor in a case under Chapter 7, 9, or 11 is a health care business, the court shall order, not later than 30 days after the commencement of the case, the appointment of an ombudsman to monitor the quality of patient care and to represent the interests of the patients of the health care business unless the court finds that the appointment of such ombudsman is not necessary for the protection of patients under the specific facts of the case. If the debtor is a health care business that provides long term care, the U.S. Trustee may appoint the State Long-Term Care Ombudsman for the state in which the case is pending. If the U.S. Trustee appoints someone else, the U.S. Trustee shall notify the State Long-Term Care Ombudsman of the name and address of the appointed ombudsman. If an ombudsman is appointed, the U.S. Trustee shall promptly file a notice of the appointment, including the name and address of the person appointed. Unless the person appointed is a State Long-Term Care Ombudsman, the notice shall be accompanied by a verified statement setting forth the person's connections with the debtor, creditors, patients, any other party in interest, their respective attorneys and accountants, the U.S. Trustee, and any person employed in the office of the U.S. Trustee. If the court has ordered that the appointment of an ombudsman is not necessary, or has ordered the termination of the appointment of an ombudsman, the court, on motion of the U.S. Trustee or a party in interest, may order the appointment at any time during the case if the court finds that the appointment of an ombudsman has become necessary to protect patients.

DUE DATE	ACTION	CODE §	RULE	EXPLANATION; TIME TO ACT
	Termination of appointment of patient care ombudsman		**Interim 2007.2(c) and (d)**	On motion of the U.S. Trustee or a party in interest, the court may terminate the appointment of a patient care ombudsman if the court finds that the appointment is not necessary for the protection of patients. The motion shall be transmitted to the U.S. Trustee and served on the debtor, the trustee, any committee elected under § 705 or appointed under § 1102, or, if the case is a Chapter 9 municipality case or a Chapter 11 reorganization case and no committee of unsecured creditors has been appointed, on the creditors included on the list filed under Rule 1007(d), and such other entities as the court may direct.
	Requirement of patient care ombudsman to report to court	**333(b)(2)**	**Interim 2015.1(a)**	Not later than 60 days after the date of appointment, and not less frequently than at 60 day intervals thereafter, the patient care ombudsman shall report to the court after notice to the parties in interest, at a hearing or in writing, regarding the quality of patient care. Unless the court orders otherwise, a patient care ombudsman, at least 10 days before making a report under § 333(b)(2), shall give notice that the report will be made to the court. The notice shall be transmitted to the U.S. Trustee, posted conspicuously at the health care facility that is the subject of the report, and served on the debtor, the trustee, all patients, and any committee elected under § 705 or appointed under § 1102 or its authorized agent, or, if the case is a Chapter 9 municipality case or a Chapter 11 reorganization case and no committee of unsecured creditors has been appointed, on the creditors included on the list filed under Rule 1007(d), and such other entities as the court may direct. The notice shall state the date and time when the report will be made, the manner in which the report will be made, and, if the report is in writing, the name, address, telephone number, email address, and website, if any, of the person from whom a copy of the report may be obtained at the debtor's expense.

DUE DATE	ACTION	CODE §	RULE	EXPLANATION; TIME TO ACT
	Requirement of patient care ombudsman to report declining or compromised care	**333(b)(3)**		If the patient care ombudsman determines that the quality of patient care is declining significantly or is otherwise being materially compromised, the ombudsman shall file with the court a motion or a written report, with notice to the parties in interest immediately upon making such determination.
	Examination of debtor's transactions with debtor's attorneys		**2017**	On motion by party in interest or on the court's own initiative, after notice and hearing, the court may determine whether any direct or indirect payment of money, or any transfer of property of debtor, made pre- or post-petition to an attorney for services rendered or to be rendered, is excessive.
	Meeting of creditors, equity security holders, and examination of debtor	**341** 343	**2003(a)**	Meeting must be held no less than 20 and no more than 40 days from order of relief. If U.S. Trustee designates location not regularly staffed by the U.S. Trustee, no more than 60 days from order of relief. At the meeting of creditors, the debtor appears and submits to examination under oath.
	Discretionary exception to requirement of meeting of creditors for pre-packaged plans at request of party in interest	**341(e)**	**Interim 2003(a)**	On the request of a party in interest and after notice and a hearing, the court may order, for cause, that the U.S. Trustee not convene a meeting of creditors or equity security holders if the debtor has filed a plan as to which the debtor solicited acceptances prior to the commencement of the case.
	Preservation by U.S. Trustee of record of § 341(a) meeting	**341**	**2003(c)**	Record must be preserved by U.S. Trustee for at least 2 years after conclusion of meeting.
	Report to the court in the event of a disputed election of a trustee or member of creditors' committee	**341**	**2003(d)**	If election is disputed, U.S. Trustee shall promptly file a report informing the court of the dispute. If no motion for the resolution of the election dispute is made to the court within 10 days after the date of the creditors' meeting, the interim trustee shall serve as the trustee in the case. For additional details concerning election of a trustee Chapter 7 case, *see* Chapter 7: Liquidation, below.

DUE DATE	ACTION	CODE §	RULE	EXPLANATION; TIME TO ACT
	Notice to individual debtors whose debts are primarily consumer debts	342(b)		Before the commencement of the case, the clerk shall give such individual written notice of the following: • a brief description of Chapters 7, 11, 12, and 13 and the general purpose, benefits, and costs of proceeding under each of those chapters; and the types of services available from credit counseling agencies; and • statements specifying that a person who knowingly and fraudulently conceals assets or makes a false oath or statement under penalty of perjury in connection with a case under this title shall be subject to fine, imprisonment, or both; and all information supplied by a debtor in connection with a case under this title is subject to examination by the Attorney General.
	Notice to creditors who have supplied addresses	342(c)		If, within the 90 days before the commencement of a voluntary case, a creditor supplies the debtor in at least 2 communications sent to the debtor with the current account number of the debtor and the address at which such creditor requests to receive correspondence, then any notice required to be sent by the debtor to such creditor shall be sent to such address and shall include such account number. The debtor shall also follow this procedure if a creditor would be in violation of applicable nonbankruptcy law by sending any such communication within such 90-day period and if such creditor supplies the debtor in the last 2 communications with the current account number of the debtor and the address at which such creditor requests to receive correspondence.

DUE DATE	ACTION	CODE §	RULE	EXPLANATION; TIME TO ACT
	Notice to creditors of presumption of abuse	342(d)	707(b) Interim 5008	In a Chapter 7 case of an individual with primarily consumer debts in which a presumption of abuse has arisen under § 707(b), the clerk shall give to creditors notice of the presumption of abuse in accordance with Rule 2002 within 10 days after the date of the filing of the petition. If the debtor has not filed a statement indicating whether a presumption of abuse has arisen, the clerk shall give notice to creditors within 10 days after the date of the filing of the petition that the debtor has not filed the statement and that further notice will be given if a later filed statement indicates that a presumption of abuse has arisen. If a debtor later files a statement indicating that a presumption of abuse has arisen, the clerk shall give notice to creditors of the presumption of abuse as promptly as practicable.
	Notice to creditors in Chapter 7 or 13 cases of individuals after service of notice of address	342(e)	Interim 2002(g)(2)[2]	In a case under Chapter 7 or 13 of a debtor who is an individual, a creditor at any time may both file with the court and serve on the debtor a notice of address to be used to provide notice in such case to such creditor. Any notice in such case required to be provided to such creditor by the debtor or the court later than 5 days after the court and the debtor receive such creditor's notice of address, shall be provided to such address.
	Notice when agreement between an entity and notice provider for manner and address of notice		2002(g)(4)	An entity and a notice provider may agree that when the notice provider is directed by the court to give a notice, the notice provider shall give the notice to the entity in the manner agreed to and at the address or addresses the entity supplies to the notice provider. That address is conclusively presumed to be a proper address for the notice. The notice provider's failure to use the supplied address does not invalidate any notice that is otherwise effective under applicable law.

[2] The Interim Rule refers to § 342(f), but the context and comment suggest that § 342(e) may have been meant, as § 342(e) is the section which applies only to individuals in chapter 7 and 13 and to notices sent by either the court or the debtor.

DUE DATE	ACTION	CODE §	RULE	EXPLANATION; TIME TO ACT
	Notice to creditors who provide an address to the court for all pending Chapter 7 and 13 cases	342(f)		An entity may file with any bankruptcy court a notice of address to be used by all the bankruptcy courts or by particular bankruptcy courts in all Chapter 7 and 13. In any Chapter 7 or 13 case, any notice required to be provided by a court to such entity after 30 days after the filing of the notice under 342(f)(1) shall be provided to the specified address unless, with respect to a particular case, a different address is specified for that case in accordance with § 342(e).
	Duties of debtor (in addition to other duties described in Code and Rules)	343 341(a)	4002	The debtor also has the following duties: • Attend and submit to examination under oath at times ordered by court; • Attend hearing on complaint objecting to discharge and testify if called as witness; • Inform trustee immediately in writing as to location of real property in which debtor has an interest, and the name and address of every person holding money or property subject to debtor's withdrawal or order, if schedule of property has not yet been filed pursuant to Rule 1007; • Cooperate with trustee in preparation of an inventory, examination of proofs of claim, and administration of estate; and • File statement of any change of debtor's address.
	Filing of state and local tax returns for corporations or partnerships	346(k)(1)	505	Unless otherwise provide in §§ 346 and 505, the time and manner of filing tax returns and the items of income, gain, loss, deduction, and credit of any taxpayer shall be determined under applicable nonbankruptcy law.
	Unclaimed property disposed of in a case under Chapter 7 or 13	347(a)		90 days after final distribution under §§ 726 or 1326, trustee shall stop payment on unpaid checks and property remaining becomes unclaimed and shall be paid into the court.
	Trustee report of creditors entitled to be paid from unclaimed property		3011	Trustee must file a list of all known names and addresses of entities and amounts they are entitled to be paid from remaining property of estate.
	Unclaimed property in a case under Chapter 11	347(b)		At expiration of time allowed for presentation of a security or the performance of any other act as a condition to participation in the distribution under any plan confirmed under §§ 1129 or 1173, unclaimed property becomes property of debtor.

DUE DATE	ACTION	CODE §	RULE	EXPLANATION; TIME TO ACT
	Effect of conversion	348(a)		Conversion of a case from one chapter to another constitutes an order for relief under the chapter to which the case is converted; except as provided in §§ 348(b) and (c), conversion does not change the date of filing of the petition, the commencement of the case, or the order for relief.
	Effect of conversion on claims	348(d)		A claim against the estate or debtor that arises after the order for relief but before conversion of a case under §§ 1112 or 1307, other than a § 503(b) claim, is treated for all purposes as if the claim had arisen immediately before the filing of the petition.
	Termination of services of trustee or examiner upon conversion	348(e)		Conversion of a case under §§ 706, 1112, 1208, or 1307 terminates the service of any trustee or examiner that is serving in the case before such conversion.
	Effect of conversion from Chapter 13 on assets and valuation	348(f)	1017 1019	Property of the estate in the converted case consists of property of the estate as of the filing date of the original petition, that remains in the possession or control of the debtor on the date of conversion; the Chapter 13 valuations of property and secured claims apply only when converted to a case under Chapter 11 or 12, but not in a case converted to a case under Chapter 7, with allowed secured claims in cases under Chapters 11 and 12 reduced to the extent they have been paid in accordance with Chapter 13 plan; and the claim of any creditor holding security as of the petition date shall continue to be secured by that security unless the full amount of such claim has been paid in full as of the conversion date. However, if debtor converts from Chapter 13 case in bad faith, property of estate in converted case consists of property of estate as of date of conversion.
	Closing of the case; final decree	350(a)	3022	In a Chapter 11 case, after estate is fully administered, the court, on its own motion or on motion of party in interest, shall enter final decree closing case. Any trustee shall be discharged by the court.
			5009	In a case under Chapter 7 or 13, if the trustee has filed final report and account and has certified that the estate is fully administered, and if no objection is filed within 30 days, there is a presumption that the estate has been fully administered, and the requirement for the court to close the case and discharge the trustee have been met.

DUE DATE	ACTION	CODE §	RULE	EXPLANATION; TIME TO ACT
	Disposal of patient records	351		If a health care business that commences a case under Chapter 7, 9, or 11 does not have sufficient funds to pay for storage of patient records, the trustee shall: (1) promptly publish notice, in 1 or more appropriate newspapers, that if patient records are not claimed with 365 days of the notification, the records will be destroyed; and (2) during the first 180 days of the 365-day period, attempt to notify patients and insurance carriers directly, advising them of the intent to dispose. If the records are not claimed after the 365-day period, the trustee shall request appropriate Federal agencies to hold the records. If the agencies refuse, the trustee then shall destroy the records.
	Automatic stay	362(a)		Automatic stay applies at commencement of case.
	Exception to the automatic stay for post-petition perfection of security interests	362(b)(3)		The filing of the petition does operate to stay any act to perfect, or to maintain or continue the perfection of, an interest in property to the extent that the trustee's rights and powers are subject to such perfection under § 546(b) or to the extent that such act is accomplished within the period provided under § 547(e)(2)(A).
	Expiration of stay on preferred ships mortgage by Secretary of Transportation	362(b)(12)		Stay expires 90 days after filing of petition as to actions brought by Secretary of Transportation under Title 46, § 31325 to foreclose on mortgage or security interest in vessels in Chapter 11 case.
	Expiration of stay on preferred ships mortgage by Secretary of Commerce	362(b)(13)		Stay expires 90 days after filing of petition as to actions brought by Secretary of Commerce under Title 46, § 31325 to foreclose on mortgage or security interests in vessel or fishing facility in Chapter 11 case.
	Exception to automatic stay for judgment of possession in residential tenancy eviction	362(b)(22)		Subject to the procedures specified in § 362(l), the filing of a petition does not operate as a stay under § 362(a)(3), of the continuation of any eviction, unlawful detainer action, or similar proceeding by a lessor against a debtor involving residential property in which the debtor resides as a tenant under a lease or rental agreement and with respect to which the lessor has obtained before the date of the filing of the bankruptcy petition, a judgment for possession of such property against the debtor.

DUE DATE	ACTION	CODE §	RULE	EXPLANATION; TIME TO ACT
	Postponement of the § 362(b)(22) exception if debtor certifies right to exercise state law right to cure in residential tenancy eviction	362(l)(1)		The exception to the stay in § 362 shall apply on the date that is 30 days after the petition date, if: (1) the debtor files with the petition and serves upon the lessor a certification under penalty of perjury that under nonbankruptcy law applicable in the jurisdiction, there are circumstances under which the debtor would be permitted to cure the entire monetary default that gave rise to the judgment for possession, after that judgment for possession was entered; and (2) the debtor (or an adult dependent of the debtor) has deposited with the clerk of the court, any rent that would become due during the 30-day period after the filing of the bankruptcy petition.
	Debtor's exercise of cure right and extinguishment of judgment for possession in residential tenancy eviction	362(l)(2)		If, within the 30-day period after the petition date, the debtor (or an adult dependent of the debtor) complies with § 522(l)(1) and files with the court and serves upon the lessor a further certification under penalty of perjury that the debtor (or an adult dependent of the debtor) has cured, under applicable nonbankrupcty law, the entire monetary default that gave rise to the judgment for possession by the lessor, § 362(b)(22) shall not apply, unless ordered to apply by the court under §§ 362(l)(3).
	Certification triggering § 362(b)(22) exception hearing	362(l)(3)(A)		If the lessor files an objection to any certification filed by the debtor under § 362(l)(1) or (2), and serves such objection upon the debtor, the court shall hold a hearing within 10 days after the filing and service of such objection to determine if the certification under §§ 362(l)(1) or (2) is true.
	Immediate application of § 362(b)(22) if landlord prevails at hearing on objection to § 362(l)(1) or (2) certification	362(l)(3)(B)		If the court upholds the objection of the lessor filed under § 362(l)(3)(A): (1) § 362(b)(22) shall apply immediately and relief from the stay shall not be required to enable the lessor to complete the process to recover full possession of the property; and (2) the clerk of the court shall immediately serve upon the lessor and the debtor a certified copy of the court's order upholding the lessor's objection.

DUE DATE	ACTION	CODE §	RULE	EXPLANATION; TIME TO ACT
	No certification filed with the petition under § 362(l)(1) or within 30 days under § 362(l)(2)	362(l)(4)		If a debtor, in accordance with § 362(l)(5), indicates on the petition that there was a judgment for possession of the residential rental property in which the debtor resides and does not file a certification under § 362(l)(1) or (2), then: (1) § 362(b)(22) shall apply immediately upon failure to file such certification, and relief from the stay shall not be required to enable the lessor to complete the process to recover full possession of the property; and (2) the clerk of the court shall immediately serve upon the lessor and the debtor a certified copy of the docket indicating the absence of a filed certification and the applicability of the exception to the stay § 362(b)(22).
	Debtor's duty to certify with the petition if judgment for possession in residential tenancy eviction and form of certification under § 362(l)	362(l)(5)(A)		Where a judgment for possession of residential property in which the debtor resides as a tenant under a lease or rental agreement has been obtained by the lessor, the debtor shall so indicate on the bankruptcy petition and shall provide the name and address of the lessor that obtained that pre-petition judgment on the petition and on any certification filed under § 362(l) using the forms specified in § 362(l)(5)(B).
	Transmittal of deposited rent	362(l)(5)(D)		The clerk of the court shall arrange for the prompt transmittal of the rent deposited in accordance with § 362(l)(1)(B) to the lessor.
	Exception to automatic stay for eviction of residential tenant eviction based on endangerment or use of controlled substances	362(b)(23)		Subject to the procedures specified in § 362(m), the filing of a petition does not operate as a stay under § 362(a)(3), of an eviction action that seeks possession of the residential property in which the debtor resides as a tenant under a lease or rental agreement based on endangerment of such property or the illegal use of controlled substances on such property, but only if the lessor files with the court, and serves upon the debtor, a certification under penalty of perjury that such an eviction action has been filed, or that the debtor, during the 30-day period preceding the date of the filing of the certification, has endangered property or illegally used or allowed to be used a controlled substance on the property.
	Effect of certification under § 362(b)(23)	362(m)(1)		Except as otherwise provided § 362(m): § 362(b)(23) shall apply on the date that is 15 days after the date on which the lessor files and serves a certification described in subsection § 362(b)(23).

DUE DATE	ACTION	CODE §	RULE	EXPLANATION; TIME TO ACT
	Effect of debtor's objection to § 362(b)(23) certification	362(m)(2)(A)		If the debtor files with the court an objection to the truth or legal sufficiency of the certification described in § 362(b)(23) and serves such objection upon the lessor, § 362(b)(23) shall not apply, unless ordered to apply by the court.
	Failure to file objection to § 362(m)(1) certification	362(m)(3)		If the debtor fails to file, within 15 days, an objection under § 362(m)(2)(A), then (1) § 362(b)(23) shall apply immediately upon such failure and relief from the stay shall not be required to enable the lessor to complete the process to recover full possession of the property; and (2) the clerk of the court shall immediately serve upon the lessor and the debtor a certified copy of the docket indicating such failure.
	Deadline for § 362(b)(23) hearing	362(m)(2)(B)		If the debtor files and serves the objection under § 362(m)(2)(A), the court shall hold a hearing within 10 days after the filing and service of such objection to determine if the situation giving rise to the lessor's certification under § 262(m)(1) existed or has been remedied.
	Hearing on landlord's certification and debtor's burden	362(m)(2)(C)		If the debtor can demonstrate to the satisfaction of the court that the situation giving rise to the lessor's certification under § 362(m)(1) did not exist or has been remedied, the stay provided under § 362(a)(3) shall remain in effect until the stay is otherwise terminated under § 362.
	Immediate effect of § 362(b)(23) if landlord prevails at hearing on certification	362(m)(2)(D)		If the debtor does not prevail at the hearing on the landlord's certification, (1) relief from the stay shall not be required to enable the lessor to proceed with the eviction; and (2) the clerk of the court shall immediately serve upon the lessor and the debtor a certified copy of the court's order upholding the lessor's certification.
	Duration of stay, generally	362(c)(1) 362(c)(2)	4001(a)	Stay of act against property continues until property is no longer property of the estate, and stay against other § 362(a) acts continues until case is closed, dismissed, or discharge is granted or denied in Chapter 7, 11, or 13, whichever is earlier.

DUE DATE	ACTION	CODE §	RULE	EXPLANATION; TIME TO ACT
	Duration of stay in a single or joint case filed by or against individual debtor under Chapter 7, 11, or 13 if a single or joint case of such debtor was pending within the preceding 1-year period, but was dismissed	362(c)(3)		If a single or joint case of such debtor was pending within the preceding 1-year period, but was dismissed, the stay with respect to any action taken with respect to a debt or property securing such debt or with respect to any lease shall terminate on the 30th day after the filing of the later case.
				On motion by a party in interest for continuance of the stay and after notice and a hearing, the court may extend the stay as to any and all creditors, after notice and a hearing completed before the expiration of the 30-day period only if the party in interest shows that the later case was filed in good faith.
				A case refiled under another chapter after dismissal under § 707(b) is not considered as a case pending within the 1-year period.
	Absence of stay in a single or joint case filed by or against individual debtor if serial filings	362(c)(4)		If 2 or more cases filed by or against that individual debtor were pending within the preceding 1-year period, but were dismissed, no stay shall go into effect as of the filing of the later case.
				If, within 30 days from the filing of the later case, a party in interest requests, the court may order the stay to take effect with respect to any or all creditors, after notice and a hearing, only if the movant demonstrates that the filing of the later case is in good faith as to the creditors to be stayed.
				If the court imposes a stay on granting such a motion, the stay becomes effective as of the date of the entry of the order.
				A case refiled under another chapter after dismissal under § 707(b) is not considered as a case pending within the 1-year period.
	Relief from stay; termination, annulment, modification of conditioning of stay	362(d)	4001(a) 9014	Court shall grant relief on request of party in interest and after notice and hearing if § 362(d) requirements are met.
				A motion for relief from an automatic stay shall be made in accordance with Rule 9014 and shall be served on any committee elected pursuant to § 705 or appointed pursuant to § 1102 or its authorized agent, or, if a Chapter 11 reorganization case and no committee of unsecured creditors has been appointed, on the creditors included on the list filed pursuant to Rule 1007(d), and on such other entities as the court may direct.

DUE DATE	ACTION	CODE §	RULE	EXPLANATION; TIME TO ACT
	Relief from stay in single asset real estate cases	**362(d)(3)**		With respect to stay of act against single asset real estate under § 362(a), court shall grant relief from stay, after request, notice, and hearing, to creditor with secured claim against such real estate, unless, not later than 90 days from order for relief (or such later date as the court determines for cause by order entered within the 90-day period) or 30 days after the court determines the debtor is subject to § 362(d)(3): • The debtor has filed a plan of reorganization that has a reasonable possibility of being confirmed within a reasonable time; or • the debtor has commenced monthly payments that may, in the debtor's sole discretion, be made from rents or other income generated before, on, or after the date of the commencement of the case by or from the property to each creditor whose claim is secured by such real estate (except creditors secured by a judgment lien or unmatured statutory lien) in an amount equal to the then applicable nondefault contract rate of interest on the value of the creditor's interest in the real estate.
	Relief from stay to prevent debtor from using petition as part of scheme to delay, hinder, or defraud creditor whose claim is secured by debtor's real property	**362(d)(4)**	**4001**	Court shall grant relief from stay if scheme involved: (A) the transfer of all or part ownership of, or other interest in, such real property without the secured creditor's consent; or (B) multiple bankruptcy filings affect such real property.

If recorded in compliance with applicable State laws governing notices of interests or liens in real property, an order entered under § 362(d)(4) shall be binding in any other bankruptcy case purporting to affect such real property filed not later than 2 years after the court's entry of the order, except that a debtor in a subsequent case may move for relief from such order based upon changed circumstances or for good cause shown. |

DUE DATE	ACTION	CODE §	RULE	EXPLANATION; TIME TO ACT
	Relief from stay; duration of stay	362(e)(1)	4001(a)	Stay is terminated with respect to any act against property of the estate after 30 days from filing the motion under Rule 4001(a) unless the court, after notice and a hearing, orders such stay continued in effect pending the conclusion of, or as a result of, a final hearing and determination under § 362(d). To continue stay pending final hearing, the court must find that there is a reasonable likelihood that the party opposing relief will prevail. If initial hearing was preliminary, final hearing must be concluded no later than 30 days after conclusion of preliminary hearing, unless 30-day period is extended with consent of parties or for a specific time which court finds is required by compelling circumstances.
		362(e)(2)		Notwithstanding § 362(e)(1), in an individual debtor case under Chapter 7, 11, or 13, the stay shall terminate on the 60th day after the motion for relief is filed, unless: (1) a final decision is rendered by the court; or (2) the 60-day period is extended by agreement of the parties or by the court for such specific period of time as the court finds is required for good cause.
	Ex parte relief from stay to avoid irreparable harm	362(f)	4001(a)(2)	Relief may be granted without prior notice under § 362(f) if requirements of Rule 4001(a)(2) are met. Party obtaining relief under § 362(f) must file verified motion or affidavit stating the basis for assertion of irreparable harm and the efforts made to give notice or why notice should not be required. After relief, the movant shall immediately give oral notice to trustee or debtor in possession and debtor and forthwith mail or otherwise transmit to adverse party or parties a copy of order. On 2 days notice to party who obtained relief, adverse party may appear and move reinstatement of stay; in that event, court must proceed expeditiously to hear and determine motion.

DUE DATE	ACTION	CODE §	RULE	EXPLANATION; TIME TO ACT
	Relief from stay; termination of stay with respect to personal property of the estate of individual debtor securing a claim, or subject to an unexpired lease	**362(h)** 365(p) 521(a)(2) 524(c) 722		The stay is terminated as to personal property in a case in which the debtor is an individual if the debtor fails to: (1) file timely a statement of intention under § 521(a)(2); or (2) indicate in such statement that the debtor either will surrender or retain such property. The stay is terminated if the debtor is retaining the property, but fails to enter into a reaffirmation agreement or to assume such unexpired lease under § 365(p), as applicable. However, the stay is not terminated if the court determines, on the motion of the trustee filed prior to expiration of the time to file a statement of intention under § 521(a)(2) (i.e., 30 days after the petition date), after notice and a hearing, that such property is of a consequential value or benefit to the estate, and orders adequate protection of creditor's interest, and orders the debtor to deliver the collateral in debtor's possession to the trustee. If the court does not so determine, stay shall terminate at conclusion of the hearing on the trustee's motion.
	Order confirming termination of stay under § 363(c)	**363(j)** 363(c)		On request of a party in interest, the court shall issue an order under § 362(c) (which provides for termination of the stay or no stay to be in effect on the occurrence of certain conditions or events) confirming that the automatic stay has been terminated.
	Stay of order granting motion for relief from stay		**400(a)(3)**	An order granting a motion for relief from an automatic stay made in accordance with Rule 4001(a)(1) is stayed until the expiration of 10 days after the entry of the order, unless the court orders otherwise.
	Use, sale, or lease of property; motion to prohibit or condition use, sale, or lease	**363(b)(1)**	**6004(a)** 2002(a)(2) 6004(e)	Trustee, after notice and hearing, may use, sell, or lease, other than in ordinary course of business, property of estate. Rule 2002(a)(2) provides for 20 day notice to parties in interest. The notice may set the date for hearing on any objections.
	Notice of motion for authority to sell property free and clear of liens or other interests		**6004(c)** 9014	Notice of motion for authority to sell property free and clear of liens or other interests must include date of hearing and objection due date, and shall be served on parties with liens or other interests in property.

DUE DATE	ACTION	CODE §	RULE	EXPLANATION; TIME TO ACT
	Requirement that proposed use, sale or lease of compliance with debtor's policy prohibiting the transfer of personally identifiable information	363(b)(1)		If the debtor in connection with offering a product or a service discloses to an individual a policy prohibiting the transfer of personally identifiable information about individuals to persons that are not affiliated with the debtor and if such policy is in effect on the date of the commencement of the case, then the trustee or debtor in possession may not sell or lease personally identifiable information to any person unless such sale or such lease is consistent with such policy. However, after appointment of a consumer privacy ombudsman, and after notice and a hearing, the court may nonetheless approve such sale or such lease giving due consideration to the facts, circumstances, and conditions of such sale or such lease; and finding that no showing was made that such sale or such lease would violate applicable nonbankruptcy law.
		363(b)(1)	Interim 2002(c)(1)	The notice of a proposed sale or lease of personally identifiable information under § 363(b)(1)(A) or (B) shall state whether the sale is consistent with a policy prohibiting the transfer of the information.
	Notice of sale subject to notification under Section 7(a) of Clayton Act	363(b)(2)		If notification is required under Section 7(a) of the Clayton Act, the required waiting period shall end on the 15th day after receipt of notice unless the period is extended under one of the provisions of § 363(b)(2)(B).
	Notice of proposed use, sale, or lease of property of gross value less than $2500	363(e)	6004(d) 9014	When all nonexempt property of estate has aggregate gross value of less than $2,500, general notice of intent is given only to all creditors, indenture trustees, committees, and U.S. Trustee. Objections in such case must be filed and served within 15 days of mailing of notice, or within time fixed by court.
	Objections to proposed use sale or lease of property.		6004(b) 9014	Objections to proposed use, sale, or lease of other property exceeding $2,500 must be filed and served not less than 5 days before date set for proposed action or within time fixed by court.
	Requirement of adequate protection of interest in property to be used, sold or leased	363(e)		On request, the court, with or without hearing, shall prohibit or condition the use, sale, or lease as is necessary to provide adequate protection.

DUE DATE	ACTION	CODE §	RULE	EXPLANATION; TIME TO ACT
	Motion to prohibit or condition the use, sale, or lease of property		**4001(a)(1)**	A motion to prohibit or condition the use, sale, or lease of property pursuant to § 363(e) shall be made in accordance with Rule 9014 and shall be served on any committee elected pursuant to § 705 or appointed pursuant to § 1102 or its authorized agent, or, if the case is a Chapter 11 reorganization case and no committee of unsecured creditors has been appointed, on the creditors included on the list filed pursuant to Rule 1007(d), and on such other entities as the court may direct.
	Ex parte motion to prohibit or condition the use, sale, or lease of property		**4001(a)(2)**	A request to prohibit or condition the use, sale, or lease of property pursuant to § 363(e) may be granted without prior notice if requirements of Rule 4001(a)(2) are met. Party obtaining relief under § 363(e) must file verified motion or affidavit stating the basis for assertion of irreparable harm and the efforts made to give notice or why notice should not be required. After relief, the movant shall immediately give oral notice to trustee or debtor in possession and debtor and forthwith mail or otherwise transmit to adverse party or parties a copy of order. On 2 days notice to party who obtained relief, adverse party may appear and move reconsideration of the order prohibiting or conditioning use, sale or lease.
	Itemized statement of property sold outside the ordinary course		**6004(f)(1)**	Sales not in the ordinary course of business may be by private sale or public auction. An itemized statement of property sold in accordance with Rule 6004(f)(1) must be filed on completion of sale, unless impracticable. If property is sold by an auctioneer, the auctioneer shall file the statement. In any other case, the trustee, debtor in possession or Chapter 13 debtor shall file the statement.
	Stay of order for use, sale or lease of property other than cash collateral		**6004(g)**	An order authorizing the use, sale, or lease of property other than cash collateral is stayed until the expiration of 10 days after entry of the order, unless the court orders otherwise. The stay does not effect that time for filing a notice of appeal under Rule 8002.

DUE DATE	ACTION	CODE §	RULE	EXPLANATION; TIME TO ACT
	No notice or approval required for use, sale or lease of property of the estate (other than cash collateral) in the ordinary course of business of debtor authorized to operate business	363(c)(1)		If business of debtor is authorized to be operated under §§ 721, 1108 or 1304, trustee may enter into transactions, including sale or lease of property of estate (other than cash collateral), in ordinary course of business, without notice or hearing, and may use property of estate in ordinary course without notice and hearing.
	Cash collateral; motion to prohibit or condition use of cash collateral	363(c)(2)		Trustee may not use, sell, or lease cash collateral unless each entity that has an interest in cash collateral consents or court, after notice and hearing, authorizes such use, sale, or lease.
			4001(b)(1)	Motion to use cash collateral must be served on any entity with interest in cash collateral, committees, or, if no committee, on Rule 1007(d) list of creditors and such others as court directs.
	Preliminary and final hearings on motion to use cash collateral		4001(b)(2)	Court may commence final hearing on motion to use cash collateral no earlier than 15 days after service of motion; if motion so requests, court may conduct preliminary hearing before such 15-day period expires, but court may authorize use of only that amount of cash collateral as is necessary to avoid immediate and irreparable harm to estate pending final hearing.
		363(f), (g) and (h)	6004(c) 9014	Notice of motion for authority to sell property free and clear of liens or other interests must include date of hearing and objection due date, and shall be served on parties with liens or other interests in property.
	Burden of proof in hearing on use, sale or lease of property	363(p)		In any hearing under § 363 for the use, sale or lease of property, the trustee has the burden of proof on the issue of adequate protection the entity asserting an interest in property has the burden of proof on the issue of the validity, priority, or extent of such interest.

DUE DATE	ACTION	CODE §	RULE	EXPLANATION; TIME TO ACT
	Credit obtained in the ordinary course as administrative expense	364(a)		If trustee is authorized to operate business under §§ 721, 1108, or 1304, trustee may obtain unsecured credit and incur unsecured debt in ordinary course of business as a § 503(b)(1) administrative expense. After notice and hearing, court may authorize trustee to obtain unsecured credit or incur unsecured debt other than § 364(a) as a § 503(b)(1) administrative expense.
	Credit obtained outside the ordinary course as administrative expense	364(b)		After notice and hearing, court may authorize trustee or debtor in possession to obtain unsecured credit or incur unsecured debt other than § 364(a) as a § 503(b)(1) administrative expense.
	Credit granted priority over other administrative expenses and/or secured by lien on unencumbered property or junior lien on encumbered property	364(c)		If trustee or debtor in possession is unable to obtain unsecured credit, court, after notice and hearing, may authorize obtaining of credit or incurring of debt with priority over all other administrative expenses and/or secured by a lien against unencumbered property or secured by junior lien.
	Credit secured by "priming" lien (lien of senior or equal rank to existing liens)	364(d)		Court, after notice and hearing, may authorize the trustee or debtor in possession to obtain credit or incur debt secured by a senior or equal lien on property of estate only if trustee is unable to obtain other credit and there is adequate protection for lien holder.
	Service of motion for authorization to obtain credit		4001(c)	Motion for authorization to obtain credit must be served on committees, or, if none, on Rule 1007(d) list of creditors and such others as court directs; motion must be accompanied by copy of agreement.
	Preliminary and final hearing on motion for authorization to obtain credit			Court may commence final hearing on motion to obtain credit no earlier than 15 days after service of motion. If motion so requests, court may conduct hearing before such 15-day period expires, but court may authorize only that amount of credit as is necessary to avoid immediate and irreparable harm to estate pending final hearing.

DUE DATE	ACTION	CODE §	RULE	EXPLANATION; TIME TO ACT
	Agreement relating to relief from stay, prohibiting or conditioning use, sale or lease of property, providing adequate protection, use of cash collateral, and obtaining credit with priming lien with consent of existing lien holder	361 362 363 364	4001(d)(1)	With respect to a motion to approve an agreement: • to provide adequate protection; • to prohibit or condition the use, sale, or lease of property; • to modify or terminate the automatic stay; • to use cash collateral; and • between the debtor and an entity that has a lien or interest in property of the estate pursuant to which the entity consents to the creation of a lien senior or equal to the entity's lien or interest in such property, • subject to Rule 4001(d)(4), the motion, notice of the motion and the time within which objections may be filed shall be served on any committee elected pursuant to § 705 or appointed pursuant to § 1102 or its authorized agent, or, if the case is a Chapter 11 reorganization case and no committee of unsecured creditors has been appointed pursuant to § 1102, on the creditors included on the list filed pursuant to Rule 1007(d), and on such other entities as the court may direct. The motion shall be accompanied by a copy of the agreement.
	Deadline to file objection to motion to approve agreement		4001(d)(2)	Unless the court fixes a different time, objections filed within 15 days of mailing of notice.
	Disposition of motion to approve agreement		4001(d)(3)	If no objection is filed, court may enter order without hearing. If an objection is filed or court determines hearing is appropriate, the court shall hold a hearing on no less than 5 days notice to objector, movant, and parties receiving service under 4001(d)(1), and other entities as the court directs.
	Waiver of requirement of further notice or hearing to approve agreement		4001(d)(4)	If court determines that motion for relief from stay, to use cash collateral or obtain authorization for credit provides sufficient notice of the material provisions of the agreement and opportunity for a hearing, the court may approve agreement between parties without further notice.

DUE DATE	ACTION	CODE §	RULE	EXPLANATION; TIME TO ACT
	Assumption or rejection of executory contracts and unexpired leases	**365(a), (b) and (c)**	**6006** **9014**	Subject to §§ 365(b), (c) and (d), the trustee or debtor in possession, on motion, and subject to the court's approval, may assume or reject any executory contract or unexpired lease of the debtor.
	Deadline to assume or reject executory contract or unexpired lease of residential real property or personal property in Chapter 7 case	**365(d)(1)**	6006 9014	In a Chapter 7 case, if the trustee does not assume or reject an executory contract or unexpired lease of residential real property or personal property within 60 days from order for relief, or within such additional time as court fixes for cause within such 60-day period, the contract, or lease is deemed rejected.
	Deadline to assume or reject executory contract or unexpired lease of residential real property or personal property in Chapter 11 or 13 case	**365(d)(2)**	6006 9014	In a case under Chapter 11 or 13, the trustee may assume or reject an executory contract or unexpired lease of residential real property or of personal property of the debtor at any time before the confirmation of a plan, but the court, on motion of any party to such contract or lease, may order the trustee to determine within a specified period of time whether to assume or reject such contract or lease.
	Performance of all obligations of unexpired lease of nonresidential real property until assumed or rejected	**365(d)(3)**		The trustee or debtor in possession shall timely perform all the obligations of the debtor, except those specified in § 365(b)(2), arising from and after the order for relief under any unexpired lease of nonresidential real property, until such lease is assumed or rejected.
	Extension of time for performance in Chapter 11 or 13 of obligations under unexpired lease of nonresidential real property	**365(d)(3)**	9006	The court may extend, for cause, the time for performance of any such obligation that arises within 60 days after the date of the order for relief, but the time for performance shall not be extended beyond such 60-day period.
	Time to assume/reject unexpired nonresidential real property lease where debtor is lessee	**365(d)(4)(A)**	9006	Subject to § 365(d)(4)(B), an unexpired lease of nonresidential real property under which the debtor is the lessee shall be deemed rejected, and the trustee shall immediately surrender that nonresidential real property to the lessor if the trustee does not assume or reject the unexpired lease by the earlier of 120 days after the date of the order for relief or the date of the entry of an order confirming a plan.

DUE DATE	ACTION	CODE §	RULE	EXPLANATION; TIME TO ACT
	Motion to assume/reject unexpired nonresidential real property lease where debtor is lessee	365(d)(4)(B)	6006 9014	The court may extend the time to assume or reject, prior to the expiration of the 120-day period, for 90 days on the motion of the trustee or lessor for cause. No further extensions may be granted without the prior written consent of the lessor; therefore, without consent, the maximum time by which the trustee must assume or reject is 210 days.
	Obligation of trustee or debtor in possession in Chapter 11 to perform obligations under unexpired lease of personal property until lease is assumed or rejected	365(d)(5)		The trustee or debtor in possession shall timely perform all obligations of the debtor, except those specified in § 365(b)(2), first arising from or after 60 days after order for relief under an unexpired lease of personal property (other than personal property leased to an individual primarily for personal, family or household purposes), until lease is assumed or rejected notwithstanding § 503(b)(1), unless court, after notice and hearing, orders otherwise.
	Right of trustee to assign an executory contract or unexpired lease of non-residential real property	365(f)(1)		Trustee may assign an executory contract or lease (notwithstanding a provision in an executory contract or unexpired lease, or in applicable law, that prohibits, restricts, or conditions the assignment of such contract or lease), so long as no termination event has occurred.
	Presumed assumption of commitment to maintain capital of insured depository institution	365(o)	6006 9014	In Chapter 11 case, trustee shall be deemed to have assumed, and must immediately cure, any deficit under or commitment to a federal depository institution, regulatory agency (or predecessor to such agency), to maintain capital of an insured depository institution.
	Termination of stay if personal property lease not assumed	365(p)(1)		The leased property ceases to be property of the estate and the automatic stay automatically terminates if a personal property lease is rejected or not timely assumed under § 365(d).

DUE DATE	ACTION	CODE §	RULE	EXPLANATION; TIME TO ACT
	Assumption of lease by Chapter 7 individual debtor	**365(p)(2)**		If the debtor in a Chapter 7 case is an individual, the debtor may notify the creditor in writing that the debtor desires to assume the lease. Thereafter, the creditor may notify the debtor that assumption is acceptable (and may condition such assumption on cure of defaults). If, within 30 days of the notice given by the creditor, the debtor notifies the creditor that the lease is assumed, the liability under the lease will be assumed by the debtor but not the estate.
	Rejection of lease of personal property in individual Chapter 11 and Chapter 13 cases if not assumed in the plan	**362(p)(3)**		If the lease is not assumed in the plan confirmed by the court, the lease is deemed rejected as of the conclusion of the hearing on confirmation. If the lease is rejected, the stay under § 362 and any co-debtor stay under § 1301 is automatically terminated with respect to the property subject to the lease.
	Discontinuing utility service for failure to provide adequate assurance of payment in Chapter 7 and 13 cases	**366(b)** **366(c)**		A utility may alter, refuse, or discontinue service if neither the trustee nor the debtor, within 20 days after the date of the order for relief, furnishes adequate assurance of payment, in the form of a deposit or other security, for service after such date.
	Discontinuing utility service for failure to provide adequate assurance of payment in Chapter 11 cases	**366(c)**		A utility may alter, refuse, or discontinue utility service, if during the 30-day period beginning on the date of the filing of the petition, the utility does not receive from the debtor or the trustee adequate assurance of payment for utility service that is satisfactory to the utility in the following forms: • cash deposit; • letter of credit; • certificate of deposit; • surety bond; • prepayment of utility consumption; and • another form of security that is mutually agreed on between the utility and the debtor or the trustee. An administrative priority shall not constitute such adequate assurance.

DUE DATE	ACTION	CODE §	RULE	EXPLANATION; TIME TO ACT
	Modification of the amount of the assurance of payment in a Chapter 11 case	366(c)(3)		On motion of any party in interest, the court may order the modification of the amount of an assurance of payment that the utility has deemed satisfactory under § 366(c)(2).
	Automatic stay does not apply to setoff by utility of prepetition deposit	366(c)(4)		Notwithstanding any other provision of law, a utility may recover or set off against a security deposit provided to the utility by the debtor before the date of the filing of the petition without notice or order of the court.

Chapter 5, Creditors, the Debtor, and the Estate, generally applies to cases filed under Chapters 7, 11, 12, 13, and (in part) Chapter 15 of the Code. The filing and allowance of claims including administrative claims, determination of tax liability and secured status of claims, the rules for priorities among and between claims, and subordination is also covered. Chapter 5 also covers the debtor's duties, exemptions, exceptions to and effect of discharge and new rules regarding debt relief agencies. Provisions regarding the debtor's estate are also in Chapter 5, including property of the estate, turnover of property, preferences, fraudulent conveyances, setoff, and abandonment.

Chapter 5: Creditors, the Debtor, and the Estate

DUE DATE	ACTION	CODE §	RULE	EXPLANATION; TIME TO ACT
	Filing of proof of claim (Chapters 7, 12 and 13)	501	3002(c)	Within 90 days after first date set for § 341(a) meeting of creditors, subject to enumerated exceptions.
	Filing of proof of claim for governmental unit	501 502(b)(9)	Interim 3002(c)(1)	Within 180 days after the date of the order for relief or, if the claim is for a tax based on a return filed under § 1308, not later than 60 days after the date on which the return was filed as required by § 1308. On motion of a governmental unit before the expiration of such period and for cause shown, the court may extend the time for filing of a claim by the governmental unit.
	Extension of time to file proof of claim for infant or incompetent person		3002(c)(2)	In the interest of justice, and if it will not unduly delay administration of the case, court may extend time to file proof of claim by infant or incompetent person, or a representative of either.
	File proof of claim for unsecured claim which arises as result of judgment if judgment is for recovery of money or property from an entity, or denies or avoids the entity's interest in property	501	3002(c)(3)	Within 30 days after judgment becomes final.
	Filing of proof of claim for claim arising from rejection of executory contract or unexpired lease	501	3002(c)(4)	Within such time as court may direct.
	In Chapter 7 case, filing of proof of claim where notice of insufficient assets was previously given by clerk pursuant to Rule 2002(e)	501	3002(c)(5)	Clerk shall notify within 90 days from mailing of notice to creditors of fact that payment of dividends appears possible.

DUE DATE	ACTION	CODE §	RULE	EXPLANATION; TIME TO ACT
	Extension of time to foreign creditor		**Interim 3002(c)(6)**	If notice of the time for filing a proof of claim has been mailed to a creditor at a foreign address, on motion filed by the creditor before or after the expiration of the time, the court may extend the time by not more than 60 days if the court finds that the notice was not sufficient under the circumstances to give the creditor a reasonable time to file a proof of claim.
	Filing of proof of claim in Chapter 11 case	501	**3003(c)(3)**	Within such time as court may fix. Notwithstanding the expiration of such time, a proof of claim may be filed to the extent and under conditions stated in Rules 3002(c)(2), (3) and (4) and Interim Rule 3002(c)(6).
	Debtor or trustee may file proof of claim on behalf of and in name of creditor if creditor fails to file timely claim	501	3004	If a creditor does not timely file a proof of claim under Rule 3002(c) or 3003(c), the debtor or trustee may file a proof of the claim within 30 days after the expiration of the time for filing claims prescribed by Rule 3002(c) or 3003(c), whichever is applicable. The Clerk shall mail notice of filing to creditor, debtor, and trustee.
	Right of entity that is or may be liable with debtor to a creditor, or has secured such creditor, to file a claim on behalf of that creditor if the creditor has not filed proof of claim pursuant to Rules 3002 or 3003(c)	501	**3005(a)**	If a creditor does not timely file a proof of claim under Rule 3002(c) or 3003(c), any entity that is or may be liable with the debtor to that creditor, or who has secured that creditor, may file a proof of the claim within 30 days after the expiration of the time for filing claims prescribed by Rule 3002(c) or Rule 3003(c), whichever is applicable. No distribution shall be made on the claim except on satisfactory proof that the original debt will be diminished by the amount of distribution.
	Extension of time to file proof of claim	501	**3003(c)(3)**	Court shall fix and for cause shown may extend the time within which proofs of claim or interest may be filed.
	Filing of evidence of transfer of claim other than for security and other than one based on a publicly traded note, bond, or debenture, after proof filed	501	**3001(e)(2)**	Transferee must file evidence of transfer. Clerk must immediately notify transferor by mail of filing of evidence of transfer, and objections are due 20 days after mailing of notification. If no objection is filed, or, if objection is filed, and court, after notice and hearing, validates transfer, order shall be entered substituting transferee for transferor.
			3001(e)(5)	Copy of objection and notice of hearing must be mailed or otherwise delivered to transferor or transferee, as appropriate, at least 30 days prior to hearing.

DUE DATE	ACTION	CODE §	RULE	EXPLANATION; TIME TO ACT
	Filing of evidence of transfer of claim for security, and other than one based on a publicly traded note, bond, or debenture, after proof filed	501	3001(e)(4)	Transferee must file evidence of the terms of the transfer. Clerk must immediately notify transferor by mail of filing of evidence of transfer, and objections are due 20 days after mailing of notification. If timely objection is filed, court, after notice and hearing, shall determine whether claim transferred for security. If no agreement regarding relative rights respecting voting, dividends, or participation in administration of estate, court shall, on motion of party in interest and after notice and a hearing, enter orders respecting these matters as appropriate.
			3001(e)(5)	Copy of objection and notice of hearing must be mailed or otherwise delivered to transferor or transferee, as appropriate, at least 30 days prior to hearing.
	Withdrawal of claim	501	3006	Creditor may withdraw as of right by filing notice of withdrawal, except that if creditor has filed proof of claim and objection is filed, or complaint is filed against creditor in an adversary proceeding, or if creditor has accepted or rejected the plan or otherwise participated significantly in case, creditor may not withdraw claim except on order of court after notice and hearing.
	Objection to claim	502(a)		Claim is deemed allowed unless timely objection filed.
		502(b)		Court determines amount of claim objected to (as of petition date) after notice and hearing.
			3007	An objection to the allowance of a claim shall be in writing and filed. A copy of the objection with notice of the hearing thereon shall be mailed or otherwise delivered to the claimant, the debtor or debtor in possession and the trustee at least 30 days prior to the hearing. If an objection to a claim is joined with a demand for relief of the kind specified in Rule 7001, it becomes an adversary proceeding.
	Reconsideration of claims	502(j)	3008	After notice and hearing.
	Limitation on amount of claim by lessor for damages resulting from termination of lease of real property	502(b)(6)	3002(c)(4)	Allowed claim may not be for more than: (a) rent reserved by lease, without acceleration, for greater of 1 year, or 15%, not to exceed 3 years of remaining term of lease following earlier of petition date and date on which lessee repossessed, or lessor surrendered, or leased property, plus (b) any unpaid rent due under lease, without acceleration.

DUE DATE	ACTION	CODE §	RULE	EXPLANATION; TIME TO ACT
	Limitation on amount of claim by employee for damages resulting from termination of employment contract	502(b)(7)		Allowed claim cannot exceed: (a) compensation provided for in contract, without acceleration, for 1 year following earlier of petition date or termination date, plus (b) any unpaid compensation due under contract, without acceleration, on earlier of above dates.
	Disallowance of certain claims for reimbursement or contribution of an entity that is liable with debtor or has secured the claim of a creditor	502(e)(1)		Subject to disallowance to the extent that: • such creditor's claim against the estate is disallowed; • such claim for reimbursement or contribution is contingent as of the time of allowance or disallowance of such claim for reimbursement or contribution; and • such entity asserts a right of subrogation to the rights of such creditor under § 509.
	Treatment of reimbursement or contribution claims which become fixed after the petition date of an entity that is liable with debtor or has secured the claim of a creditor	502(e)(2)		Subject to disallowance under § 502(e)(1), a claim that becomes fixed after commencement of case shall be determined, and shall be allowed under §§ 502(a), (b), or (c), or disallowed under § 502(d), the same as if such claim had become fixed before the petition date.
	Allowance of ordinary course "gap" claims (which arise after the petition is filed but before the order for relief) in involuntary cases	502(f) 507(a)(3)		Determined as of date claim arises, and allowed under §§ 502(a), (b), or (c), or disallowed under §§ 502(d) or (e), the same as if claim had arisen before petition date. However, such claims are third priority claims under § 507(a)(3).
	Determination of claim arising from rejection, under § 365, or under a Chapter 11 or 13 plan, of an executory contract or unexpired lease of debtor that has not been assumed	502(g)		Determined, and allowed under §§ 502(a), (b), or (c), or disallowed under §§ 502(d) or (e), the same as if claim had arisen before petition date.
	Determination of claim arising from recovery of property under §§ 522, 550, or 553	502(h)		Determined and allowed under §§ 502(a), (b), or (c), or disallowed under §§ 502(d) or (e), the same as if claim had arisen before petition date.
	Determination of claim that does not arise until after commencement of case for a tax entitled to priority under § 507(a)(8)	502(i) 507(a)(8)		Determined and allowed under §§ 502(a), (b), or (c), or disallowed under §§ 502(d) or (e), the same as if claim had arisen before petition date. However, such claims are eighth priority claims under § 507(a)(8).

DUE DATE	ACTION	CODE §	RULE	EXPLANATION; TIME TO ACT
	Reduction of claim based in whole or part on unsecured consumer debt of creditor who unreasonably refused to negotiate alternative payment schedule proposed by credit counseling agency	502(k)		On motion of the debtor, the claim may be reduced by not more than 20% if: • the offer was made at least 60 days before the date of the filing of the petition; • provided for payment of at least 60% of the amount of the debt over a period not to exceed the repayment period of the loan, or a reasonable extension thereof; and • no part of the debt under the alternative repayment schedule is nondischargeable.
	Request for payment of administrative claim	503(a)		An entity may timely file a request for payment of an administrative expense, or may tardily file such request if permitted by the court for cause. Deadline is established pursuant to any order of the court.
	Exemption of requirement to file request for payment of administrative expense by governmental unit for certain taxes incurred by the estate	503(b)(1)(D)		A governmental unit shall not be required to file a request for the payment of taxes incurred by the estate, tax attributable to an excessive carryback allowance adjustment received by the estate or any fine, penalty or reduction in credit related to these taxes.
	Request for payment of administrative claim filed before conversion of a case	503(a)	1019(6)	A request for payment of an administrative expense incurred before conversion of the case is timely if it is filed either before conversion or within time fixed by the court.
	Allowance of administrative claims, generally	503(b)		After notice and hearing.
	Allowance of administrative claim for rejection of previously assumed non-residential real property lease	503(b)(7)		Allowed administrative claim equal to the sum of all monetary obligations due, excluding those arising from or relating to a failure to operate or a penalty provision, for the period of 2 years following the later of the rejection date or the date of actual turnover of the premises, without reduction or setoff for any reason whatsoever except for sums actually received or to be received from an entity other than the debtor.
				The claim for remaining sums due for the balance of the term of the lease shall be a claim under § 502(b)(6).

DUE DATE	ACTION	CODE §	RULE	EXPLANATION; TIME TO ACT
	Allowance of administrative claim for value of any goods received by the debtor within 20 days before the petition date	503(b)(9)		Administrative (second) priority if the goods are received by the debtor within 20 days before the petition date and sold in the ordinary course of the debtor's business.
	Limitation on allowance of retention bonuses for insiders	503(c)(1)		A retention bonus for an insider may neither be allowed nor paid unless: • the transfer or obligation is essential to retention of the person because the individual has a bona fide job offer from another business at the same or greater rate of compensation; • the services provided by the person are essential to the survival of the business; and • either: (1) the amount is not greater than 10 times the amount of the mean transfer or obligation of a similar kind given to nonmanagement employees for any purpose during the calendar year in which the transfer is made or the obligation is incurred; or (2) if no such similar transfers or obligations during such calendar year, the amount of the transfer or obligation is not greater than an amount equal to 25% of the amount of any similar transfer or obligation made to or incurred for the benefit of such insider for any purpose during such calendar year. The court must make findings based on evidence on the record.
	Limitation on allowance of severance for insiders	503(c)(2)		Severance for an insider may neither be allowed nor paid unless: • the payment is part of a program that is generally applicable to all full-time employees; and • the amount of the payment is not greater than 10 times the amount of the mean severance pay given to nonmanagement employees during the calendar year in which the payment is made.
	Determination of right to tax refund	505(a)(2)(B)		Court cannot determine before earlier of 120 days after refund is requested or determination by governmental unit of the request.

DUE DATE	ACTION	CODE §	RULE	EXPLANATION; TIME TO ACT
	Address for services of requests for § 505(b)(2) expedited review of tax returns	**505(b)(1)**	**Interim 5003(e)**	The clerk shall maintain a list under which a governmental unit responsible for the collection of taxes within the district may designate an address for service of requests under § 505(b)(2).
				The United States, state, territory, or local governmental unit responsible for the collection of taxes within the district in which the case is pending may file a statement designating an address for service of requests under § 505(b), and the designation shall describe where further information concerning additional requirements for filing such requests may be found.
				The mailing address in the register is conclusively presumed to be a proper address for the governmental unit, but the failure to use that mailing address does not invalidate any notice that is otherwise effective under applicable law.
				If such governmental unit does not designate an address and provide such address to the clerk, the request may be served at the address for the filing of a tax return or protest with the appropriate taxing authority.
	Discharge of liability of estate, the trustee, the debtor, and any successor to the debtor for tax incurred during administration of estate (absent fraud)	**505(b)(2)**		A trustee may request a determination of any unpaid liability of the estate for any tax incurred during the administration of the case by submitting a tax return for such tax and a request for such a determination to the governmental unit charged with responsibility for collection or determination of such tax at the address and in the manner designated in § 505(b)(1). Unless such return is fraudulent, or contains a material misrepresentation, the estate, the trustee, the debtor, and any successor to the debtor is discharged from any liability for such tax if the trustee pays tax shown on the return and governmental unit does not notify trustee, within 60 days after request, that return was selected for examination, or does not notify trustee of tax due within 180 days after request.
				If governmental unit does notify the trustee, the tax liability is discharged by payment of the tax as determined by the court, after notice and a hearing, after the completion of the governmental unit's examination, or by payment of the tax liability as determined by the governmental unit.

DUE DATE	ACTION	CODE §	RULE	EXPLANATION; TIME TO ACT
	Determination by court of value of claim secured by lien on property in which estate has an interest	506(a)	3012 7001	Valuation of the secured claim upon motion of a party in interest and after notice (which includes notice to the holder of the secured claim) and hearing. An adversary proceeding must be commenced for the determination of the validity, priority or extent of a lien.
	First priority for domestic support obligations	507(a)(1)		Allowed unsecured claims for domestic support obligations that, as of the date of the filing of the petition in a case under this title, are owed to or recoverable by a spouse, former spouse, or child of the debtor, or such child's parent, legal guardian, or responsible relative without regard to whether the claim is filed by such person or is filed by a governmental unit on behalf of such person. Allowed unsecured claims for domestic support obligations that, as of the date of the filing of the petition, are assigned by a spouse, former spouse, child of the debtor, or such child's parent, legal guardian, or responsible relative to a governmental unit (unless such obligation is assigned voluntarily). Allowed unsecured claim by the spouse, former spouse, child, parent, legal guardian, or responsible relative of the child for the purpose of collecting the debt) or are owed directly to or recoverable by a governmental unit under applicable nonbankruptcy law.
	Second priority for administrative expenses; exception to subordination to domestic support obligations	507(a)(2) 507(a)(1)(C)		The administrative expenses of the trustee allowed under §§ 503(b)(1)(A), (2), and (6) shall be paid before payment of domestic support obligations under §§ 507(a)(1)(A) and (B), to the extent that the trustee administers assets that are otherwise available for the payment of such claims.

DUE DATE	ACTION	CODE §	RULE	EXPLANATION; TIME TO ACT
	Fourth priority for wage, salary and commission claims, including vacation, severance and sick leave pay, earned by individuals and certain corporations	507(a)(4)		Earned within earlier of 180 days prior to petition or date of cessation of business, not to exceed $10,000 for: • (a) wages, salaries, or commissions, including vacation, severance, and sick leave pay earned by an individual; or • (b) sales commissions earned by an individual or a corporation with only 1 employee, acting as an independent contractor in sale of goods or services for debtor in ordinary course of debtor's business if, and only if, during 12 months preceding the petition date, at least 75% of the amount that the individual or a corporation earned by acting as an independent contractor in sale of goods or services was earned from debtor.
	Fifth priority for contributions to an employee benefit plan	507(a)(5)		Arising from services rendered within earlier of 180 days prior to petition or date of cessation of business, but only, for each such plan, the number of employees covered by such plan multiplied by $10,000 less the sum of the aggregate amount paid to such employees under § 507(a)(4) plus the aggregate amount paid by estate on behalf of such employees to any other employee benefit plan
	Eighth priority for certain allowed tax claims	507(a)(8)		See below.
	Taxes on income or gross receipts	507(a)(8)(A)		For taxable year ending on or before the petition date, for which a return, if required, is last due, including extensions, after 3 years before the petition date or assessed within 240 days before the filing of the petition, which 240 day period is subject to adjustments as specified in § 507(a)(8)(A).
	Allowed property tax claim	507(a)(8)(B)		Incurred before commencement of case and last payable within 1 year before petition date.
	Allowed employment tax claim	507(a)(8)(D)		Earned pre-petition and return last due within 3 years before petition date.
	Allowed excise tax claim	507(a)(8)(E)		Pre-petition transaction and return last due within 3 years before petition date or if no return required, transaction occurred during 3 years prior to petition.

DUE DATE	ACTION	CODE §	RULE	EXPLANATION; TIME TO ACT
	Allowed customs duty claim	507(a)(8)(F)		Merchandise imported for consumption within 1 year prior to petition, or covered by an entry within 1 year pre-petition, or entered for consumption within 4 years pre-petition but unliquidated on that date for reasons identified in § 508(a)(8)(F)(iii).
	Equitable subordination of claims or interests	510(c)	7001	After notice and a hearing, the court may: (1) under principles of equitable subordination, subordinate for purposes of distribution all or part of an allowed claim to all or part of another allowed claim or all or part of an allowed interest to all or part of another allowed interest; or (2) order that any lien securing such a subordinated claim be transferred to the estate. An adversary proceeding must be commenced for the subordination an allowed clam or interest, except when a Chapter 9, 11 or 13 plan provides for such subordination, in which case the propriety of the subordination may be determined as part of the confirmation proceedings.
	Interest rate on allowed tax claim	511 1129(a)		If any provision requires the payment of interest on a tax claim or on an administrative expense tax or the payment of interest to enable a creditor to receive the present value of the allowed amount of a tax claim, the rate of interest shall be the rate determined under applicable non-bankruptcy law. In the case of taxes paid under a confirmed plan, the rate of interest shall be determined as of the calendar month in which the plan is confirmed.

DUE DATE	ACTION	CODE §	RULE	EXPLANATION; TIME TO ACT
	Duty of Debtor to file Schedule of Assets and Liabilities, schedule of Income and Expenditures and Statement of Affairs and other documents in voluntary case	**521(a)(1)** **521(c)**	**1007(a),** **Interim** **1007(b) and** **Interim** **1007(c)**	The schedules and statements and other documents specified in Rule 1007(b)(1), (4),(5), and (6), prepared as prescribed by the appropriate Official Forms, if any: shall be filed with the petition in a voluntary case, or if the petition is accompanied by a list of all the debtor's creditors and their addresses, within 15 days thereafter, except as otherwise provided in Rule 1007 (d), (e), and (h). The documents specified in Rule 1007(b)(1) are: • schedules of assets and liabilities; • a schedule of current income and expenditures; • a schedule of executory contracts and unexpired leases; • a statement of financial affairs; • copies of all payment advices or other evidence of payment, if any, with all but the last four digits of the debtor's social security number redacted, received by the debtor from an employer within 60 days before the filing of the petition (new); and • a record of any interest that the debtor has in an education IRA or qualified State tuition program of the type specified in § 521(c). In an involuntary case the schedules and statements, other than the statement of intention, shall be filed by the debtor within 15 days after entry of the order for relief. Schedules and statements filed prior to the conversion of a case to another chapter shall be deemed filed in the converted case unless the court directs.
	Extension for filing schedules and statements	**521(a)(1)**	**Interim** **1007(c)**	Except as otherwise provided in § 1116(3) pertaining to small business cases, any extension of time for the filing of the schedules and statements may be granted only on motion for cause shown and on notice to the United States trustee and to any committee elected under § 705 or appointed under § 1102 of the Code, trustee, examiner, or other party as the court may direct. Notice of an extension shall be given to the U.S. Trustee and to any committee, trustee, or other party as the court may direct.

DUE DATE	ACTION	CODE §	RULE	EXPLANATION; TIME TO ACT
	Extension for filing schedules and statements in a small debtor Chapter 11 case	**521(a)(1) 1116(3)**	**Interim 1007(c)**	Same procedure as for other debtors, but absent extraordinary and compelling circumstances, the court may not extend the time for filing the statements and schedules in a small business case beyond a date which is 30 days after the order for relief.
	Documents to be provided by an individual debtor in Chapter 7, 11, or 13 cases	**521(a)(1)(B)(iv) and (e)(2)(A)**	**Interim 4002(b)(1), (2) and (3)**	The following information must be brought to the meeting of creditors: • Personal Identification: a picture identification issued by a governmental unit, or other personal identifying information that establishes the debtor's identity; and evidence of social security number(s), or a written statement that such documentation does not exist; and • Financial information: evidence of current income such as the most recent pay stub; unless the trustee or the United States trustee instructs otherwise, statements for each of the debtor's depository and investment accounts, including checking, savings, and money market accounts, mutual funds and brokerage accounts for the time period that includes the date of the filing of the petition; and documentation of monthly expenses claimed by the debtor when required by § 707(b)(2)(A) or (B). At least 7 days before the first date set for the meeting of creditors under § 341, the debtor shall provide to the trustee a copy of the debtor's federal income tax return for the most recent tax year ending immediately before the commencement of the case and for which a return was filed, including any attachments, or a transcript of the tax return, or provide a written statement that the documentation does not exist or is not in the debtor's possession.
	Debtor's duty to provide requesting creditor with tax return for most recent tax year	**521(e)(2)(A)(ii)**	**Interim 4002(b)(4)**	If a creditor, at least 15 days before the first date set for the meeting of creditors under § 341, requests a copy of the debtor's tax return that is to be provided to the trustee under Interim Rule 4002(b)(3), the debtor shall provide to the requesting creditor a copy of the return, including any attachments, or a transcript of the tax return, or provide a written statement that the documentation does not exist or is not in the debtor's possession at least 7 days before the first date set for the meeting of creditors under § 341.

DUE DATE	ACTION	CODE §	RULE	EXPLANATION; TIME TO ACT
	Dismissal for failure to provide tax return to requesting creditor	**521(e)(2)(B) and (C)**		If the debtor fails to timely provide the trustee or requesting creditors the tax return or transcript specified in § 521(e)(2), the court shall dismiss the case unless the debtor demonstrates that the failure to so comply is due to circumstances beyond the control of the debtor.
	Chapter 7 individual debtor's statement of intention of surrender or retention of property of the estate	**521(a)(2)(5)**	**Interim 1007(b)(2)**	Within 30 days after the date of the filing of the Chapter 7 petition or on or before the date of the meeting of creditors, whichever is earlier, or within such additional time as the court, for cause, within such period fixes, an individual debtor in a Chapter 7 case shall file a statement of intention as required by § 521(a) prepared as prescribed by the appropriate Official Form. A copy of the statement shall be served on the trustee and the creditors named in the statement on or before the filing of the statement.
	Chapter 7 debtor must perform intention with respect to property set forth in statement of intention	**521(a)(2)(B)**		Within 30 days after the first date set for the meeting of creditors, or within such additional time as the court, for cause, within such 30 day period, fixes.
	Individual debtor's appearance at discharge hearing	**521(a)(5) 524(d)**		As scheduled by court.
	Individual Chapter 7 debtor's duty to surrender personal property as to which creditor has allowed claim for purchase price secured by an interest in such property	**521(a)(6) 524(c) 722**		Unless within 45 days of the first meeting of creditors, debtor enters into a reaffirmation agreement under § 524(c) or redeems such property from the security interest under § 722.\n\nIf debtor fails to act within such 45 day period, the stay is terminated with respect to such personal property and is no longer property of the estate, unless after notice and a hearing on motion of trustee filed before expiration of 45 day period, court finds that property is of consequential value to estate, orders adequate protection to creditor, and orders debtor to deliver collateral to trustee.
		521(b)(3)	**Interim 1007(b)(3) and (c)**	Unless the United States trustee has determined that the credit counseling requirement of § 109 does not apply in the district, an individual debtor must file the certificate and debt repayment plan, if any, required by § 521(b), a certification under § 109(h)(3), or a request for a determination by the court under § 109(h)(4).

DUE DATE	ACTION	CODE §	RULE	EXPLANATION; TIME TO ACT
	Request by creditor of copy of petition, schedules or statement of affairs by an individual in a Chapter 7 or 13 case	**521(e)(1)**		If a creditor files with the court at any time a request to receive a copy of the petition, schedules, and statement of financial affairs filed by the debtor, then the court shall make such petition, such schedules, and such statement available to such creditor.
	Individual debtor's duty to file Federal tax returns with the court in Chapter 7, 11 or 13 case	**521(f)(4) (1)(2) and (3)**		At the request of court, U.S. Trustee, or party in interest, at the same time filed with the taxing authority. The debtor may elect to file a transcript rather than the tax return. This applies to any tax return: • for each year ending while the case is pending; • that had not been filed with such authority as of the commencement of the case and that was subsequently filed for any tax year of the debtor ending in the 3-year period ending on the date of the commencement of the case; and • a copy of each amendment or transcript of amendment to any of the foregoing.
	Duty of Chapter 13 creditor to file statement of income and expenditures during the tax year recently concluded	**521(f)(4) 521(g)(1)**		In a case under Chapter 13, on the date that is either 90 days after the end of such tax year or 1 year after the date of the commencement of the case, whichever is later, if a plan is not confirmed before such later date; and annually after the plan is confirmed and until the case is closed, not later than the date that is 45 days before the anniversary of the confirmation of the plan, the debtor shall file with the court a statement, under penalty of perjury, of the income and expenditures of the debtor during the tax year of the debtor most recently concluded before such statement is filed, and of the monthly income of the debtor.
	Dismissal of voluntary case of an individual under Chapter 7 or 13 case for debtor's failure to comply with § 521(a)(1) within 45 days after the filing of the petition	**521(i)(1) 521(i)(2)** 521(a)(1)		If the individual debtor fails to file all the information required by § 521(a)(1) within 45 days after the filing of the petition, the case shall be automatically dismissed effective on the 46th day after the petition date. Any party in interest may request the court to enter an order dismissing the case. If requested, the court shall enter an order of dismissal not later than 5 days after such request, which dismissal is nonetheless effective on the 46th day after the petition date.

DUE DATE	ACTION	CODE §	RULE	EXPLANATION; TIME TO ACT
	Request by debtor for extension of the period for complying with § 521(a)(1)	**521(i)(3)**		Upon request of the debtor made within 45 days after the date of the filing of the petition, the court may allow the debtor an additional period of not to exceed 45 days to file the information required under § 521(a)(1) if the court finds justification for extending the period for the filing.
	Declination to dismiss for failure to file payment advices upon request of trustee	**521(i)(4)**		On the motion of the trustee filed before the expiration of the applicable period of time specified in §§ 521(i)(1), (2), or (3), and after notice and a hearing, the court may decline to dismiss the case if the court finds that the debtor attempted in good faith to file all the information required by § 521(a)(1)(B)(iv) and that the best interests of creditors would be served by administration of the case.
	Dismissal or conversion for debtor's failure to file tax returns	**521(j)**		If debtor fails to file return within 90 days after taxing authority requests return to be filed, court shall covert or dismiss case, whichever is in best interest of creditors and estate.
	Qualification as exempt property (individual debtors only)	**522(b)**	4003(a) 1007	A debtor shall list the property claimed as exempt under § 522 on the schedule of assets and liabilities to be filed under Rule 1007. If the debtor fails to claim exemptions within the time for filing such schedule, a dependent may file the exemptions within 30 days thereafter.
	Election of state or federal exemptions by individual debtor	**522(b)(1)**	4003(a) 1007	An individual debtor may exempt from property of the estate the property listed in §§ 522(b)(2) (federal exemptions of § 522(d)) or (3) (state exemptions plus non-bankruptcy federal exemptions).
	Election of state or federal exemptions by married couples filing joint petition	**522(b)(1)**		In joint cases filed by or against debtors who are husband and wife, and whose estates are ordered to be jointly administered under Rule 1015(b), one debtor may not elect to exempt property listed in § 522(b)(2) and the other debtor may not elect to exempt property listed in § 522(b)(3). If the parties cannot agree on the alternative to be elected, they shall be deemed to elect § 522(b)(2), where such election is permitted under the law of the jurisdiction where the case is filed.

DUE DATE	ACTION	CODE §	RULE	EXPLANATION; TIME TO ACT
	Domicile of debtor for applicable state exemptions, when electing state law exemption	522(b)(3)(A)		Subject to §§ 522(o) and (p), in addition to the exemption of any property that is exempt under Federal law, other than § 524(d), exemption under the State or local law that is applicable on the date of the filing of the petition at the place in which the debtor's domicile has been located for the 730 days immediately preceding the date of the filing of the petition, or if the debtor's domicile has not been located at a single State for such 730-day period, the place in which the debtor's domicile was located for 180 days immediately preceding the 730-day period or for a longer portion of such 180-day period than in any other place. If the effect of the domiciliary requirement under § 522(b)(3)(A) renders the debtor ineligible for any exemption, the debtor may elect to exempt property that is specified § 522(d).
	Avoidance of certain liens on exempt property	522(f)	4003(d) 9014	On motion of the debtor, the debtor may avoid the fixing of a lien on an interest of the debtor in property to the extent that such lien impairs an exemption and is a judicial lien, other than a judicial lien that secures a domestic support obligation, or a nonpurchase money security interest in the consumer goods, tools of trade or health aids described in § 522(f)(1)(B), subject to the limitation in § 522(f)(3).
	Exemption of recoveries of the trustee	522(g)	4003(a) 1009(a)	The debtor may exempt under that the trustee recovers under §§ 510(c)(2), 542, 543, 550, 551, or 553 to the extent that the debtor could have exempted such property under § 522(b) if such property had not been transferred, if: (1) such transfer was not a voluntary transfer of such property by the debtor and the debtor did not conceal such property; or (2) the debtor could have avoided such transfer under § 522(f)(1)(B).
	Debtor's right to commence avoidance action	522(h)		The debtor may avoid a transfer of property of the debtor or recover a setoff to the extent that the debtor could have exempted such property under § 522(g)(1) if: (1) such transfer is avoidable by the trustee under §§ 544, 545, 547, 548, 549, or 724(a) or recoverable by the trustee under § 553; and (2) the trustee does not attempt to avoid such transfer.

DUE DATE	ACTION	CODE §	RULE	EXPLANATION; TIME TO ACT
	Objection to exemptions	522(l)	Interim 4003(b)(1)	Except for an objection based on § 522(q), a party in interest may file an objection to the list of property claimed as exempt within 30 days after the meeting of creditors held under § 341(a) is concluded or within 30 days after any amendment to the list or supplemental schedules is filed, whichever is later. The court may, for cause, extend the time for filing objections if, before the time to object expires, a party in interest files a request for an extension.
	Objection to exemption under § 522(q)	522(q)	Interim 4003(b)(2)	An objection to a claim of exemption based on § 522(q) shall be filed before the closing of the case. If an exemption is first claimed after a case is reopened, an objection shall be filed before the reopened case is closed.
	Limitation on exemption of residence, burial plot or homestead under state exemptions	522(p)		Except as provided in § 522(p)(2) and §§ 544 and 548, as a result of electing § 522(b)(3)(A) to exempt property under State or local law, a debtor may not exempt any amount of interest that was acquired by the debtor during the 1215-day period preceding the petition date that exceeds in the aggregate $125,000 in value in: (1) real or personal property that the debtor or a dependent of the debtor uses as a residence; (2) a cooperative that owns property that the debtor or a dependent of the debtor uses as a residence; (3) a burial plot for the debtor or a dependent of the debtor; or (4) real or personal property that the debtor or dependent of the debtor claims as a homestead. Any amount of such interest does not include any interest transferred from a debtor's previous principal residence (which was acquired prior to the beginning of such 1215-day period) into the debtor's current principal residence, if the debtor's previous and current residences are located in the same State. The amendment adding § 522(p) applies to all bankruptcy cases filed on or after April 20, 2005, the enactment date.

DUE DATE	ACTION	CODE §	RULE	EXPLANATION; TIME TO ACT
	Limitation on exemption of residence, burial plot or homestead under state exemptions by persons convicted of certain felonies or liable for certain debts for fraud or intentional torts	**522(q)**		As a result of electing § 522(b)(3)(A) to exempt property under State or local law, a debtor may not exempt any amount of an interest in property described in § 522(p)(1) which exceeds in the aggregate $125,000 if: (1) the court determines, after notice and a hearing, that the debtor has been convicted of a felony (as defined in 18 USC § 3156 which under the circumstances demonstrate that the filing of the case was an abuse of the Code); (2) if the debtor owes a debt arising from the securities fraud and other activity described in § 522(q)(1)(B); (3) if the debtor owes a debt arising from any civil remedy under section 18 USC § 1964; or (4) if the debtor owes a debt arising from any criminal act, intentional tort, or willful or reckless misconduct that caused serious physical injury or death to another individual in the preceding 5 years. The amendment adding § 522(q) applies to all bankruptcy cases filed on or after April 20, 2005, the enactment date.
	Duty of an individual Chapter 11 debtor or Chapter 13 debtor who elects state law exemptions on property described in § 522(p)(1) that exceeds $125,000	**522(q)**	**Interim 1007(b)(8)**[1]	If an individual debtor in a Chapter 11 or 13 case has claimed an exemption under § 522(b)(3)(A) in an amount in excess of the amount set out in § 522(q)(1) in property of the kind described in § 522(p)(1), the debtor shall file a statement as to whether there is pending a proceeding in which the debtor may be found guilty of a felony of a kind described in § 522(q)(1)(A) or found liable for a debt of the kind described in § 522(q)(1)(B).
	Deadline for an individual Chapter 11 debtor or Chapter 13 debtor who elects state law exemptions on property described in § 522(p)(1) that exceeds $125,000 to file Interim Rule 1007(b)(8) statement		**Interim 1007(c)**[2]	The statement required by Interim Rule 1007(b)(8) shall be filed by the debtor not earlier than the date of the last payment made under the plan or the date of the filing of a motion for entry of a discharge under §§ 1141(d)(5)(B) or 1328(b).

[1] This modification to the Interim Rules was proposed on October 13, 2005. Check your court's local rule to determine whether this Interim Rule was adopted as part of its local rules.

[2] This modification to the Interim Rules was proposed on October 13, 2005. Check your court's local rule to determine whether this Interim Rule was adopted as part of its local rules.

DUE DATE	ACTION	CODE §	RULE	EXPLANATION: TIME TO ACT
	Non-dischargeability of debt of individual debtor for certain tax or a customs duty	523(a)(1)		A debt is not dischargeable to the extent such debt is for a tax or custom duty: • entitled to priority pursuant to §§ 507(a)(3) or 507(a)(8); • with respect to which a return was not filed or given; • with respect to which a return was filed or given or given after it was due (including extensions) and within 2 years before the petition date; or • with respect to which the debtor made a fraudulent return or willfully attempted to evade or defeat the tax.
	Non-dischargeability of debt of individual debtors obtained by fraud	523(a)(2)(A) 523(c)	Interim 4007(c)	A debt is not dischargeable to the extent such debt is for money, property, services, or an extension, renewal, or refinancing of credit, to the extent obtained, by false pretenses, a false representation, or actual fraud, other than a statement respecting the debtor's or an insider's financial condition.
	Presumption of non-dischargeability of certain consumer debts for "luxury goods or services"	523(a)(2)(C)(I)		For purposes of § 523(a)(2)(A), consumer debts owed to a single creditor and aggregating more than $500 for "luxury goods or services" incurred by an individual debtor on or within 90 days before the order for relief are presumed to be non-dischargeable.
	Presumption of non-dischargeability of certain cash advances	523(a)(2)(C)(II)		For purposes of § 523(a)(2)(A), cash advances aggregating more than $750 that are extensions of consumer credit under an open-end credit plan obtained by an individual debtor on or within 70 days before the order for relief are presumed to be non-dischargeable.
	Non-dischargeability of debt of individual debtors obtained by use of false financial statement	523(a)(2)(B) 523(c)	Interim 4007(c)	A debt is not dischargeable to the extent such debt is for money, property, services, or an extension, renewal, or refinancing of credit, to the extent obtained by use of a statement in writing: (1) that is materially false; (2) respecting the debtor's or an insider's financial condition; (3) on which the creditor to whom the debtor is liable reasonably relied; and (4) that the debtor caused to be made or published with intent to deceive.
	Non-dischargeability of debt of individual debtors for fraud or defalcation in a fiduciary capacity	523(a)(4) 523(c)	Interim 4007(c)	A debt is not dischargeable to the extent such debt is for fraud or defalcation while acting in a fiduciary capacity, embezzlement, or larceny.

DUE DATE	ACTION	CODE §	RULE	EXPLANATION: TIME TO ACT
	Non-dischargeability of domestic support obligations	**523(a)(5)** **101(14)**		A debt is not dischargeable to the extent such debt is for a domestic support obligation. A debt which constitutes a domestic support obligation includes such debts that accrue before, on, or after the date of the order for relief. For the definition of a domestic support obligation, *see* Chapter 1: General Provisions
	Non-dischargeability of debt of individual debtors for willful and malicious injury	**523(a)(6)** **523(c)**	Interim 4007(c)	A debt is not dischargeable to the extent such debt is for willful and malicious injury by the debtor to another entity or to the property of another entity.
	Non-dischargeability of debts of individual debtor for a fine, penalty, or forfeiture to a governmental unit	**523(a)(7)**		A debt is not dischargeable to the extent such debt is for a fine, penalty, or forfeiture payable to and for the benefit of a governmental unit, and is not compensation for actual pecuniary loss. However a tax penalty is discharged unless it relates to a tax which is non-dischargeable under § 523(a)(1) or is imposed with respect to a transaction or event that occurred before three years before the petition date.
	Non-dischargeability of student loan debt	**523(a)(8)**		Unless excepting such debt from discharge would impose an undue hardship on the debtor and the debtor's dependents, a debt is not dischargeable to the extent such debt is for: (1) an educational benefit overpayment or loan made, insured, or guaranteed by a governmental unit or made under any program funded in whole or in part by a governmental unit or nonprofit institution; (2) an obligation to repay funds received as an educational benefit, scholarship or stipend; or (3) any other educational loan that is a qualified education loan.
	Non-dischargeability of debt of individual debtor for postpetition homeowners fees and assessments	**523(a)(16)**		A debt is not dischargeable to the extent such debt is for a fee or assessment that becomes due and payable after the order for relief to a membership association with respect to the debtor's interest in a unit that has condominium ownership, in a share of a cooperative corporation, or a lot in a homeowners association, for as long as the debtor or the trustee has a legal, equitable, or possessory ownership interest in such unit, such corporation, or such lot, but nothing in § 523(a)(16) shall except from discharge the debt of a debtor for a membership association fee or assessment for a period arising before entry of the order for relief.

DUE DATE	ACTION	CODE §	RULE	EXPLANATION: TIME TO ACT
	Deadline for filing complaint to determine whether debts are dischargeable for debts covered by § 523(c)	**523(c)** 523(a)(2), (4) and (6)	**Interim 4007(c)** 7001	Except as provided in Rule 4007(d), a complaint to determine the dischargeability of a debt under § 523(c) shall be filed no later than 60 days after the first date set for the meeting of creditors under § 341(a). The court shall give all creditors no less than 30 days notice of the time so fixed in the manner provided in Rule 2002. On motion of any party in interest, after hearing on notice, the court may for cause extend the time. The motion shall be filed before the time has expired.
	Time for filing complaint for determination of dischargeability of a debt other than under § 523(c)		**4007(b)**	Complaint to determine the dischargeability of a debt other than a debt covered by § 523(c) may be filed at any time.
	Effect of a discharge	**523(a)(1) and (2)** 727 1141 1328		A discharge: (1) voids any judgment at any time obtained, to the extent that such judgment is a determination of the personal liability of the debtor with respect to any debt discharged under §§ 727, 1141 or 1328, whether or not discharge of such debt is waived; and (2) operates as an injunction against the commencement or continuation of an action, the employment of process, or an act, to collect, recover or offset any such debt as a personal liability of the debtor, whether or not discharge of such debt is waived.
	Effect of discharge on community claims against property acquired after commencement of the case and exception for non-dischargeable claims	**524(a)(3)**		A discharge operates as an injunction against the commencement or continuation of an action, the employment of process, or an act, to collect or recover from, or offset against, property of the debtor of the kind specified in § 541(a)(2) that is acquired after the commencement of the case, on account of any allowable community claim. However, this injunction does not apply to a community claim that is excepted from discharge under §§ 523, or 1328(a)(1), or that would be so excepted, determined in accordance with §§ 523(c) and (d), in a case concerning the debtor's spouse commenced on the date of the filing of the petition in the debtor's case, whether or not discharge of the debt based on such community claim is waived.

DUE DATE	ACTION	CODE §	RULE	EXPLANATION: TIME TO ACT
	Exception to injunction of § 524(a)(3) when spouse is or would be denied a discharge	524(b) 727(a)	4004(a) 7001	The injunction under § 524(a)(3) does not apply (a) if debtor's spouse is a debtor in a case commenced within 6 years of petition date of the debtor's case, and court does not grant debtor's spouse a discharge in that case, or (b) if the court would not grant discharge to debtor's spouse in case under Chapter 7 if commenced on date of filing of debtor's petition and that determination is made by court within time and in manner provided for determination under § 727.
	Reaffirmation agreement based on dischargeable debt	524(c) 524(d) 524(k) 1141(d)(4)	4008	A reaffirmation agreement is enforceable only to extent enforceable under applicable nonbankruptcy law and only if: (1) the agreement was made before granting of discharge under §§ 727, 1141, or 1328; (2) the debtor received disclosures described in § 524(k) at or before the time the debtor signed agreement; (3) the agreement has been filed with court and, if applicable, accompanied by the required attorney declaration or affidavit; (4) debtor has not rescinded agreement prior to the discharge or within 60 days after agreement filed with court, whichever is later; (5) if the debtor was not represented by an attorney when the agreement was negotiated, the hearing under § 524(d) is held complied with when the debtor was not represented by an attorney when the agreement was negotiated (disclosures and determination by the court); and (6) if individual not represented by counsel, court makes § 524(c)(6) findings (the agreement will not impose undue hardship and is in debtor's best interest). Under circumstances where a hearing is required to approve a reaffirmation agreement, a motion must be filed for approval of the reaffirmation agreement.
	Statement of total income and expenses	524(k)(6)	4008	The debtor shall sign and date the statement in support of the reaffirmation agreement, as specified in § 524(k)(6), prior to filing with the court. The debtor's statement required under § 524(k) shall be accompanied by a statement of the total income and total expense amounts stated on Schedules I and J. If there is a difference between the income and expense amounts, the accompanying statement shall include an explanation of any difference.

DUE DATE	ACTION	CODE §	RULE	EXPLANATION: TIME TO ACT
	Presumption of undue hardship at hearing	524(m)	4008 4004(c)(1)(J)	Until 60 days after a reaffirmation agreement is filed with the court (or such additional period as the court, after notice and a hearing and for cause, orders before the expiration of such period), it shall be presumed that such agreement is an undue hardship on the debtor if the debtor's monthly income less the debtor's monthly expenses as shown on the debtor's completed and signed statement in support of the agreement under § 524(k)(6)(A) is less than the scheduled payments on the reaffirmed debt. This presumption shall be reviewed by the court. The presumption may be rebutted in writing by the debtor if the statement includes an explanation that identifies additional sources of funds to make the payments. If the presumption is not rebutted to the satisfaction of the court, the court may disapprove such agreement. No agreement shall be disapproved without notice and a hearing to the debtor and creditor. Such hearing shall be concluded before the entry of the debtor's discharge.
	Discharge hearing	524(d)	Interim 4008	Not more than 30 days following the entry of an order granting or denying a discharge or confirming a plan in a Chapter 11 reorganization case concerning an individual debtor and on not less than 10 days notice to the debtor and the trustee, the court may hold a hearing as provided in § 524(d).
	Reaffirmation hearing (individuals only)	524(d) 524(k)	Interim 4008	May be at discharge hearing, only if discharge granted and § 524(d) requirements are met. A motion by the debtor for approval of a reaffirmation agreement shall be filed before or at the hearing. The debtor's statement required under § 524(k) shall be accompanied by a statement of the total income and total expense amounts stated on Schedules I and J. If there is a difference between the income and expense amounts stated on Schedules I and J and the statement required under § 524(k), the statement shall include an explanation of any difference.

DUE DATE	ACTION	CODE §	RULE	EXPLANATION: TIME TO ACT
	Issuance by court of injunction in connection with order confirming Chapter 11 plan of reorganization, to supplement the discharge injunction in cases where debtor is defendant in asbestos liability cases	524(g)		After notice and hearing, a court that enters an order confirming a plan of reorganization under Chapter 11 may issue, in connection with such order, an injunction in accordance with § 524(g) to supplement the injunctive effect of a discharge. Notwithstanding § 524(e), such an injunction may bar any action directed against a third party who is identifiable from the terms of such injunction (by name or as part of an identifiable group) and is alleged to be directly or indirectly liable for the conduct of, claims against, or demands on the debtor under the circumstances of § 524(g)(4)(A)(ii). If the requirements of § 524(g)(2)(B) are met and the order confirming the plan of reorganization was issued or affirmed by the district court that has jurisdiction over the reorganization case, then after the time for appeal of the order that issues or affirms the plan the injunction shall be valid and enforceable and may not be revoked or modified by any court except through appeal to the court of appeals in accordance with § 524(g)(6).
	Notice and transmission of documents to entities subject to an injunction under a plan		3017(f)	For details, *see* Chapter 11: Reorganization.
	Form of order confirming plan, including content of supplemental injunction		3020(c)(1)	For details, *see* Chapter 11: Reorganization.
			3020(c)(2) and (3)	For details, *see* Chaper 11: Reorganization.
	Deadlines for disclosure and statement by to be made by debt relief agency under §§ 526(a)(2) and (b)	527(a)(2)		A debt relief agency providing bankruptcy assistance to an assisted person shall provide, in addition to providing the notice required to be given under § 342(b)(1), shall give a clear and conspicuous written notice containing the information required by § 526(a)(2) not later than 3 business days after the first date on which a debt relief agency first offers to provide any bankruptcy assistance services to an assisted person. At the same time, the debt relief agency shall provide each assisted person the statement set forth in § 527(b).

DUE DATE	ACTION	CODE §	RULE	EXPLANATION; TIME TO ACT
	Required information provided by debt relief agency to assisted person regarding financial information	527(b)		A debt relief agency providing bankruptcy assistance to an assisted person, to the extent permitted by nonbankruptcy law, shall provide each assisted person at the time required for the notice required in § 527(a)(1) (reasonably sufficient information in a clear and conspicuous writing) on how to provide all of the information the assisted person is required to provide under § 521, including information on the valuation of assets, determination of income, "means testing," disposable income in Chapter 13 cases, completion of schedule of creditors, and the determination of exemptions and their value.
	Required retention of notices provided by debt relief agency under § 527(a)	527(d)		A debt relief agency must maintain a copy of notices required under § 527(a) for 2 years after notice given.
	Deadline for debt relief agency to execute written contract with assisted person	528(a)		Not later than 5 business days after the first date on which such agency provides any bankruptcy assistance services to an assisted person, but prior to such assisted person's petition under this title being filed, a debt relief agency shall execute a written contract with such assisted person that explains clearly and conspicuously describes the services, fees and terms of payment. The agency shall provide the assisted person with a copy of the fully executed and completed contract.
	Determination of what property of the debtor becomes property of the estate	541(a)		Determined as of commencement of case, which is when bankruptcy estate is created.

DUE DATE	ACTION	CODE §	RULE	EXPLANATION; TIME TO ACT
	When interests of debtor in property received post-petition become property of the estate	**541(a)(5)**		Any interest in property that would have been property of the estate if such interest had been an interest of the debtor on the date of the filing of the petition, and that the debtor acquires or becomes entitled to acquire within 180 days after such date: (1) by bequest, devise, or inheritance; (2) as a result of a property settlement agreement with the debtor's spouse, or of an interlocutory or final divorce decree; or (3) as a beneficiary of a life insurance policy or of a death benefit plan.
	Filing of supplemental schedule if debtor acquires or becomes entitled to acquire any interest in § 541(a)(5) property	**541(a)(5)**	**1007(h)**	Debtor shall within 10 days after the information comes to the debtor's knowledge or within such further time as the court may allow, file a supplemental schedule. If any of the property is claimed as exempt, debtor shall claim the exemptions in the supplemental schedule. The duty to file supplemental schedules for § 541(a)(5) property continues notwithstanding the closing of the case, except that schedule need not be filed in a Chapter 11 or 13 case for property acquired after entry of order confirming Chapter 11 plan or discharging debtor in Chapter 13 case.
	Exclusion from property of estate of funds placed in education individual retirement account (as defined in IRC § 530(b)(1))	**541(b)(5)**		Property of the estate does not include funds placed in an education individual retirement account (as defined in § 530(b)(1) of the Internal Revenue Code of 1986) not later than 365 days before the date of the filing of the petition only if: (1) the designated beneficiary of such account was a child, stepchild, grandchild, or step-grandchild of the debtor for the taxable year for which funds were placed in such account; (2) to the extent that such funds are not pledged or promised to any entity in connection with any extension of credit and are not excess contributions (as described in IRC § 4973(e)); and (3) in the case of funds placed in all such accounts having the same designated beneficiary not earlier than 720 days nor later than 365 days before such date, only so much of such funds as does not exceed $5,000.

DUE DATE	ACTION	CODE §	RULE	EXPLANATION; TIME TO ACT
	Exclusion from property of funds used to purchase a tuition credit or certificate or contributed to education IRA	541(b)(6)		Property of the estate does not include funds used to purchase a tuition credit or certificate or contributed to an account in accordance with IRC § 529(b)(1)(A) under a qualified State tuition program not later than 365 days before the petition date: (1) only if the designated beneficiary of the amounts paid or contributed was a child, stepchild, grandchild, or step-grandchild of the debtor for the taxable year for which funds were paid or contributed; (2) with respect to the aggregate amount paid or contributed to such program having the same designated beneficiary, only so much as does not exceed the total contributions permitted under IRC § 529(b)(7) with respect to such beneficiary, as adjusted pursuant to § 541(a)(6)(B); and (3) in the case of funds paid or contributed to such program having the same designated beneficiary not earlier than 720 days nor later than 365 days before such date, only so much of such funds as does not exceed $5,000.
	Exclusion from property of funds withheld or contributed for contribution to pension plan, deferred compensation plan or tax deferred annuity	541(b)(7)		Property of the estate does not include any amount withheld by an employer from the wages of employees for payment or received by an employer from an employee for payment as contributions to: • an employee benefit plan subject to title I of ERISA or under an employee benefit plan which is a government plan under IRC § 414(d) or a deferred compensation plan under IRC § 457 or a tax-deferred annuity under IRC § 403(b); or • a health insurance plan regulated by State law.
	Exclusion from property of estate of certain interests in cash or cash equivalents constituting proceeds of sale by debtor of a money order	541(b)(9)		If sale was made by debtor 14 days or less before the petition date, and under agreement with money order issuer that prohibits commingling of such proceeds with property of the debtor, (notwithstanding that, contrary to agreement, debtor has actually commingled), unless money order issuer had not taken action, prior to petition date, to require compliance with the prohibition.

DUE DATE	ACTION	CODE §	RULE	EXPLANATION; TIME TO ACT
	Turnover of property of estate	542(a)	7001	An entity, other than a custodian, in possession, custody, or control, during the case, of property that the trustee may use, sell, or lease under § 363, or that the debtor may exempt under § 522, shall deliver to the trustee, and account for, such property or the value of such property, unless such property is of inconsequential value or benefit to the estate. An action to recover money, other than a proceeding to compel the debtor to deliver property to the trustee, is an adversary proceeding commenced by a complaint.
	Turnover of property of estate constituting recorded information	542(e)		Court may order, after notice and hearing, subject to any applicable privilege.
	Turnover of property by a custodian; accounting; examination of administration	543		Delivery must be made on the date that the custodian acquires knowledge of the commencement of the case and an accounting must be filed with the court. (Note that a custodian who is assignee for benefit of debtor's creditors that was appointed or took possession more than 120 days before petition date may be excused from delivering property upon court order and after notice and hearing).
			6002(a)	Custodian must promptly file and transmit to U.S. Trustee a report and account with respect to property of estate and administration thereof.
			6002(b)	On filing and transmittal of report and account and examination, and after notice and hearing, the court shall determine propriety of administration, including reasonableness of disbursements.
	Trustee's status as lien creditor to void unperfected interests in property of the estate	544(a)	7001	The trustee shall have, as of the commencement of the case, and without regard to any knowledge of the trustee or of any creditor, the rights and powers of, or may avoid any transfer of property of the debtor or any obligation incurred by the debtor that is voidable by the lien creditors described in §§ 544(a)(1),(2) and (3).
	Trustee's strong arm power based on rights of unsecured creditor with an allowed claim	544(b)(1)	7001	The trustee may avoid any transfer of an interest of the debtor in property or any obligation incurred by the debtor that is voidable under applicable law by a creditor holding an unsecured claim that is allowable under § 502 or that is not allowable only under § 502(e).

DUE DATE	ACTION	CODE §	RULE	EXPLANATION; TIME TO ACT
	Safe harbor for certain transfers to qualified religious or charitable entity subject to fraudulent conveyance actions and preemption of such actions	544(b)(2)		Section 544(b)(1) shall not apply to a transfer of a charitable contribution (as that term is defined in § 548(d)(3)) that is not avoidable under § 548(a)(1)(B), by reason of § 548(a)(2). Any claim by any person to recover a transferred contribution described in the preceding sentence is preempted by the commencement of the case.
	Deadline for bringing an action or proceeding under §§ 544, 545, 547, 548, or 553	546(a)		An action under §§ 544, 545, 547, 548, or 553 may not be commenced after the earlier of: (a) the later of 2 years after entry of order for relief or 1 year after appointment or election of first trustee under §§ 702, 1104, 1163, or 1302 if such appointment or election occurs before expiration of such period; or (b) the time case is closed or dismissed.
	Limitations on avoiding powers of trustee under §§ 544, 545, and 549	546(b)		Rights and powers of trustee are subject to any generally applicable law that: (1) permits perfection of interest in property to be effective against an entity that acquires rights in the property before perfection; or (2) provides for the maintenance or continuation of perfection to be effective against an entity that acquires rights in property before date on which action is taken to effect such maintenance or continuation. If applicable law requires seizure of property or commencement of action to achieve perfection, or maintenance or continuation of perfection, and seizure or commencement has not occurred by date of petition, interest in the property shall be perfected postpetition by notice within the time fixed for such seizure or commencement.
	Requirements for creditor who is seller of goods to assert reclamation rights	546(c)		The trustee's rights and powers to avoid an interest in property are subject to the reclamation rights of a seller as described in § 546(c). However, a seller may not seek reclamation of goods unless seller demands reclamation in writing: (1) not later than 45 days after the date of receipt of goods by debtor; or (2) not later than 20 days after commencement of case, if the 45-day period expires after the commencement of the case.

DUE DATE	ACTION	CODE §	RULE	EXPLANATION; TIME TO ACT
	Requirements for creditor who is producer of grain sold to a grain storage facility or who is a U.S. fisherman who sold fish to a fish processing facility to assert reclamation rights	**546(d)**		In the case of a seller who is a producer of grain sold to a grain storage facility, owned or operated by the debtor, in the ordinary course of such seller's business or in the case of a U.S. fisherman who has caught fish sold to a fish processing facility owned or operated by the debtor in the ordinary course of such fisherman's business, the trustee's avoidance powers are subject to any statutory or common law right to reclaim such grain or fish if the debtor has received such grain or fish while insolvent. However the producer or fisherman may not seek reclamation unless such producer or fisherman demands, in writing, reclamation of such grain or fish before 10 days after receipt thereof by the debtor.
	Limitations on avoiding powers of trustee against margin payments, settlement payments, or swap agreement transfers	**546(e)** **546(f)** **546(g)**		Notwithstanding the rights and powers of a trustee under §§ 544(a), 545, 547, 549, and 553, the trustee cannot avoid designated margin or settlement payments or transfers under a swap agreement, described in §§ 546(e), (f) and (g), that are made before commencement of case, except under § 548(a)(1)(A).
	Trustee's or debtor in possession's right to return goods and receive credit	**546(h)**		Notwithstanding the rights and powers of a trustee under §§ 544(a), 545, 547, 549, and 553, if the court determines on a motion by the trustee made not later than 120 days after the date of the order for relief under Chapter 11, after notice and a hearing, that a return is in the best interests of the estate, the debtor, with the consent of a creditor and subject to the prior rights of holders of security interests in such goods or the proceeds, may return goods shipped to the debtor by the creditor before the commencement of the case, and the creditor may offset the purchase price of such goods against any claim of the creditor against the debtor that arose before the commencement of the case.
	Preservation of warehouseman's lien against avoidance	**546(i)**		Notwithstanding §§ 545(2) and (3), the trustee may not avoid a warehouseman's lien for storage, transportation, or other costs incidental to the storage and handling of goods.

DUE DATE	ACTION	CODE §	RULE	EXPLANATION; TIME TO ACT
	Limitations on avoiding powers of trustee against master netting agreement	546(j)		Notwithstanding the rights and powers of a trustee under §§ 544(a), 545, 547, 549, and 553, the trustee may not avoid a transfer made by or to a master netting agreement participant under or in connection with any master netting agreement or any individual contract covered thereby that is made before the commencement of the case, except under § 548(a)(1)(A), and except to the extent that the trustee could otherwise avoid such a transfer made under an individual contract covered by such master netting agreement.
	Date tax debt is incurred for preference purposes	547(a)(4)		Debt for a tax is incurred on the day when the tax is last payable without penalty, including any extension.
	Preference period under § 547(b)	547(b)(4)		The preference period covers transfers made on or within 90 days before petition to any creditors, or, for insiders, also between 90 days and 1 year before the petition date.
	Exception to avoidance for timely perfected purchase money security interests	547(c)(3)		The trustee may not avoid under § 547 a transfer that creates a security interest in property acquired by the debtor: (1) to the extent such security interest secures new value that was (a) given at or after the signing of a security agreement that contains a description of such property as collateral; (b) given by or on behalf of the secured party under such agreement to enable the debtor to acquire such property and in fact so used by the debtor; and (2) that is perfected on or before 30 days after the debtor receives possession of such property.
	Limitation on avoidance of perfected security interests in inventory or a receivable or proceeds of either ("floating lien collateral")	547(c)(5)		The trustee may not avoid under § 547 that creates a perfected security interest in inventory or a receivable or the proceeds of either, except to the extent that the aggregate of all such transfers to the transferee caused a reduction, as of the date of the filing of the petition and to the prejudice of other creditors holding unsecured claims, of any amount by which the debt secured by such security interest exceeded the value of all security interests for such debt on the later of: (1) (a) with respect to non-insiders, 90 days before the petition date; or (b) with respect to insiders, 1 year before the petition date; or (2) the date on which new value was first given under the security agreement creating such security interest.

DUE DATE	ACTION	CODE §	RULE	EXPLANATION; TIME TO ACT
	Date of perfection of transfer	547(e)(1)(A)		For real property other than fixtures, but including interest of seller or purchaser under contract for sale of real property, is perfected when a bona fide purchaser from debtor against whom applicable law permits such transfer to be perfected cannot acquire an interest superior to interest of transferee.
		547(e)(1)(B)		For fixture or property other than real property, perfection is when creditor on simple contract cannot acquire a judicial lien superior to interest of transferee.
	Date of transfer is for purposes of § 547	547(e)(2)		For purposes of § 547, a transfer is made: (1) at time the transfer takes effect, if the transfer is perfected at or within 30 days after such time, except as provided in § 547(c)(3)(B); (2) at the time the transfer is perfected, if transfer is perfected after 30 days; or (3) immediately before filing of petition, if transfer is not perfected at later of commencement of case or 30 days after transfer takes effect.
	Presumption of insolvency for purposes of § 547	547(f)		For the purposes of § 547, the debtor is presumed insolvent on and during 90 days immediately preceding petition date.
	Safe harbor for transfers under an alternative repayment schedule	547(h)		The trustee may not avoid a transfer if such transfer was made as a part of an alternative repayment schedule between the debtor and any creditor created by an approved nonprofit budgeting and credit counseling agency.
	Amendment confirming rejection of *Deprizio*[3] holding	547(i)		If the trustee avoids under § 547(b) a transfer made between 90 days and 1 year before the date of the filing of the petition, by the debtor to an entity that is not an insider for the benefit of a creditor that is an insider, such transfer shall be considered to be avoided under § 547 only with respect to the creditor that is an insider.

[3] *Levit v. Ingersoll Rand Fin. Corp.*, 874 F.2d 1186 (7th Cir. 1986).

DUE DATE	ACTION	CODE §	RULE	EXPLANATION; TIME TO ACT
	Transfers subject to fraudulent conveyance actions	548(a)(1)	7001	The trustee may avoid any transfer (including any transfer to or for the benefit of an insider under an employment contract) of an interest of the debtor in property, or any obligation (including any obligation to or for the benefit of an insider under an employment contract) incurred by the debtor, that was made or incurred on or within 2 years before the petition date, if the transfer was an actual fraud defined in § 548(a)(1)(A) or a constructive fraud defined in § 548(a)(1)(B), including a transfer to or for the benefit of an insider, or incurred such obligation to or for the benefit of an insider, under an employment contract and not in the ordinary course of business. The amendment to this provision increasing the period to 2 years applies to all bankruptcy cases filed on or after one year after the date of enactment, which is April 20, 2006. For cases filed prior to such date, the provision applies to transfers made or obligations incurred within 1 year of the petition. The amendment adding insider transfers under employment contracts applies to all bankruptcy cases filed on or after April 20, 2005, the enactment date.
	Safe harbor for certain transfers to qualified religious or charitable entity subject to fraudulent conveyance actions	548(a)(2)		A transfer of a charitable contribution to a qualified religious or charitable entity or organization shall not be considered to be a transfer covered under § 548(a)(1)(B) in any case in which: (1) the amount of that contribution does not exceed 15% of the gross annual income of the debtor for the year in which the transfer of the contribution is made; or (2) even if greater than 15%, if the transfer was consistent with the practices of the debtor in making charitable contributions.

DUE DATE	ACTION	CODE §	RULE	EXPLANATION; TIME TO ACT
	Avoidance of transfers of partnership debtor to general partner	548(b)		The trustee of a partnership debtor may avoid any transfer of an interest of the debtor in property, or any obligation incurred by the debtor, that was made or incurred on or within 2 years before the petition date, to a general partner in the debtor, if the debtor was insolvent on the date such transfer was made or such obligation was incurred, or became insolvent as a result of such transfer or obligation. This provision applies to all bankruptcy cases filed on or after one year after the date of enactment, which is April 20, 2006. For cases filed prior to such date, the provision applies to transfers made or obligations incurred within 1 year of the petition date.
	Defense of good faith transferee to the extent of value	548(c)		Except to the extent that a transfer or obligation is voidable under §§ 544, 545, or 547, a transferee or obligee of such a transfer or obligation that takes for value and in good faith has a lien on or may retain any interest transferred or may enforce any obligation incurred to the extent that such transferee or obligee gave value to the debtor in exchange for such transfer or obligation.
	Date a transfer is deemed made for purposes of § 548	548(d)(1)		Transfer is deemed made when transfer is so perfected that a bona fide purchaser cannot acquire superior interest, but if transfer is not perfected pre-petition, transfer is deemed made immediately before petition filed.
	Transfers made by debtor to self-settled trust with actual intent to hinder, delay or defraud	548(e)		The trustee may avoid any transfer of an interest of the debtor in property that was made on or within 10 years before the date of the filing of the petition if: (1) such transfer was made by the debtor to a self-settled trust or similar device; (2) the debtor is a beneficiary of such trust or similar device; and (3) the debtor made such transfer with actual intent to hinder, delay, or defraud any entity to which the debtor was or became indebted at or after the time of the transfer. This provision applies to all bankruptcy cases filed on or after April 20, 2005.

DUE DATE	ACTION	CODE §	RULE	EXPLANATION; TIME TO ACT
	Avoidance of unauthorized postpetition transactions	**549(a)**	7001	The trustee may avoid a transfer of property of the estate that occurs after the commencement of case, not authorized by the Code or the court or authorized only under §§ 303 or 542(c), subject to exceptions in §§ 549(b) and (c).
	In involuntary case, safe harbor against avoidance of certain "gap" transfers made after the commencement of an involuntary case but before order for relief	**549(b)**		In an involuntary case, the trustee can not avoid a transfer under § 549(a) to the extent any value, including services, but not including satisfaction or securing of a prepetition debt, is given after commencement of case in exchange for transfer, notwithstanding notice or knowledge of the case by the transferee.
	Time for bringing avoidance actions regarding postpetition transactions under §§ 549(a) and (b)	**549(d)**		Must be commenced before earlier of: (1) 2 years after the date of the transfer; or (2) the time the case is closed or dismissed.
	Inability of trustee to recover property under § 550(a) from non-insider transferee in § 547(b) avoidance actions	**550(c)**		If transfer made between 90 days and 1 year pre-petition is avoided under § 547(b) and was made for benefit of a creditor that at time of transfer was an insider, trustee may not recover under § 550(a) from a transferee that is not an insider.
	Deadline for bringing actions against transferees under § 550	**550(f)**	7001	Must be commenced before earlier of 1 year after the date of the avoidance of the underlying transfer or the time the case is closed or dismissed.
	Ability of creditor with allowed claim to offset a mutual prepetition debt	**553(a)(2), (3)**		Subject to §§ 362 and 363, the Code does not affect any right of a creditor to offset a mutual debt owing by such creditor to the debtor that arose before the commencement of the case against claim of such creditor against the debtor that arose before the commencement of the case (which is not disallowed), except to the extent the claim was transferred by an entity other than the debtor to the creditor: (1) after the commencement of the case; (2) after 90 days before the filing of the petition and while debtor was insolvent; or (3) the debt owed to the debtor was incurred by the creditor after 90 days before the filing of the petition, while the debtor was insolvent, and for the purpose of obtaining a right of setoff. These exceptions to the preservation of the right of setoff do not apply to the kinds of setoff described in §§ 362(b)(6), 362(b)(7), 362(b)(17), 362(b)(27), 555, 556, 559, 560, or 561.

DUE DATE	ACTION	CODE §	RULE	EXPLANATION; TIME TO ACT
	Ability of trustee to recover amounts offset by creditors	553(b)		Except as noted in § 553(b)(1) (the same exceptions as applicable under §§ 553(2) and (3)), if a creditor offsets a mutual debt owing to the debtor against a claim owed by the debtor on or within 90 days before the petition date, the trustee may recover from the creditor the amount offset to the extent that any insufficiency on the date of the setoff is less than the insufficiency on the later of: (1) 90 days before the petition date; or (2) the first date during the 90-day pre-petition period on which there is an insufficiency.
	Presumption of insolvency for § 553 purposes	553(c)		Debtor presumed insolvent on and during the 90 days immediately preceding date of petition.
	Abandonment of property of estate by trustee	554	6007(a)	The trustee may abandon property that is burdensome to the estate or of inconsequential value; after notice to U.S. Trustee, all creditors, indenture trustees, and committees and a hearing. Objections must be filed and served within 15 days of mailing of the notice, or within time fixed by court; if timely objection made, court may grant only after notice and hearing.
	Abandonment on motion of party in interest	554(b)	6007(b)	Abandonment proceedings may also be commenced by a party filing a motion requesting abandonment.
	Automatic abandonment	554(c)		Unless the court orders otherwise, any property scheduled under § 521(a)(1) not otherwise administered at the time of the closing of a case is automatically abandoned to the debtor and administered for the purposes of § 350 (closing of the case).
	Expedited determination of interests in, and abandonment or other disposition of grain assets	557(c)(1) 557(f)		On court's own motion, court may, and on request of trustee or an entity that claims an interest in grain or the proceeds of grain, the court shall expedite the procedures for determination of interests in and the disposition of grain and the proceeds of grain, by establishing a timetable having a duration not greater than 120 days for the completion of the § 557(d) procedure. The 120-day time period may be extended by the court for cause under § 557(f).

Chapter 7, Liquidation, includes sections dealing with appointment and election of a trustee, conversion, dismissal, distribution scheme, discharge, and liquidation provisions for stockbrokers, commodity brokers, and clearing banks.

Chapter 7: Liquidation

DUE DATE	ACTION	CODE §	RULE	EXPLANATION; TIME TO ACT
	Appointment of Chapter 7 interim trustee	**701(a)**	2001	Promptly after the order for relief is entered.
	Appointment of interim Chapter 7 trustee before order for relief in involuntary case; bond; turnover of records and property and filing of final report and account	701 **303(g)**	**2001(a)**	At any time following commencement of involuntary liquidation case and before order for relief, on motion of a party in interest, after notice to the debtor and a hearing, if necessary to preserve the property of the estate or prevent loss to the estate.
	Requirement of bond and specification of reasons for appointment and duties	**303(i)**	**2001(b)**	An interim trustee may not be appointed unless a bond is furnished by movant in an amount approved by the court for costs, attorneys' fees and damages under 303(i). The order appointing the interim trustee shall specify the reasons for the appointment and the trustee's duties.
			2001(d)	Following qualification of trustee under § 702, unless otherwise ordered, the interim trustee must forthwith deliver to trustee all records and property in possession or control, and, within 30 days file a final report and account.
	Termination of interim trustee	**701(b)**		Service terminates when a trustee is elected or designated under § 702 and qualifies under § 322.
	Election of Chapter 7 trustee	**702** 322(a)	**2006** **2008**	At § 341 meeting, qualified creditors may elect trustee if an election is requested by qualified creditors. If trustee is not elected, the interim trustee shall serve as the trustee. Only non-insider creditors with allowable, undisputed, fixed liquidated, unsecured claims and non-priority claims are entitled to vote. The U.S. Trustee immediately notifies the person selected how to qualify and, if applicable, the amount of the trustee's bond.

DUE DATE	ACTION	CODE §	RULE	EXPLANATION; TIME TO ACT
	Acceptance or rejection of office by selected trustee		**2008** 2010	Trustee that has filed a blanket bond pursuant to Rule 2010 that does not notify court and U.S. Trustee in writing of rejection of the office within 5 days after receipt of notice of selection is deemed to have accepted the office. All others selected as trustees must notify court and U.S. Trustee in writing of acceptance of office within 5 days after receipt of notice of selection or are deemed to have rejected the office.
	Data required from holders of multiple proxies		**2006(e)**	At any time before voting commences at any § 341(a) meeting, or at any other time as court may direct, a holder of 2 or more proxies shall file and transmit to the U.S. Trustee a verified list of proxies to be voted and a verified statement of pertinent facts and circumstances in connection with execution and delivery of each proxy, including information set forth in Rule 2006(e).
	Enforcement of restrictions on solicitation		**2006(f)**	On motion, or its own initiative, court may determine whether there has been a failure to comply with provisions of Rule 2006 or any other impropriety in connection with solicitation or voting of a proxy, and, after notice and hearing, court may reject any proxy for cause, vacate any order entered in consequence of the voting of any proxy which should have been rejected, or take any other appropriate action.
	Duty of trustee to file reports, if business of debtor is authorized to be operated	**704(a)(8)**	2015(a)	If business of debtor is authorized to be operated, the trustee shall file with the court, the U.S. Trustee, and any governmental unit charged with responsibility for collection or determination of any tax arising out of such operation, periodic reports and summaries of the operation of the business, including a statement of receipts and disbursements, a statement of amounts of deductions for all taxes required to be withheld or paid for and in behalf of employees and the place where monies are deposited, and such other information as the U.S. Trustee or the court requires.

DUE DATE	ACTION	CODE §	RULE	EXPLANATION; TIME TO ACT
	Duty of trustee to provide notice holder of claim for a domestic support obligation and State child support agency	704(a)(10) 704(c)		If there is a claim for a domestic support obligation, the trustee shall: (1) provide written notice to the holder of the claim of such claim and of the right of such holder to use the services of the State child support enforcement agency for assistance in collecting child support during and after the case; (2) include in the notice the address and telephone number of such State child support enforcement agency; and (3) include in the notice an explanation of the rights of such holder to payment of such claim under Chapter 7 chapter.
				The trustee shall also provide written notice to such State child support enforcement agency of such claim; and include in the notice the name, address, and telephone number of the holder of the claim.
				At such time as the debtor is granted a discharge, the trustee shall provide written notice to the holder and to the State child support enforcement agency of: (1) the granting of the discharge; (2) the last recent known address of the debtor; (3) the last recent known name and address of the debtor's employer; and (4) the name of each creditor that holds a claim that is not discharged under §§ 523(a)(2), (4), or (14A) or was reaffirmed by the debtor under § 524(c).
	Duty of U.S. Trustee to file with court a statement as to whether individual debtor's case would be presumed to be an abuse under § 707(b)	704(b)(1) 707(b)		Not later than 10 days after the date of the first meeting of creditors.
	Duty to file motion to dismiss or convert or reasons motion is not appropriate	704(b)(2) 707(b)		If the U.S. Trustee files such a statement, the U.S. Trustee is required to file a motion to dismiss or convert, or file a statement as setting forth the reasons why the U.S. Trustee does not believe such a motion is appropriate.
	Duty of trustee or debtor in possession to file a complete inventory of property of debtor		2015(a)	In a Chapter 7 case the trustee shall file and transmit to the U.S. Trustee a complete inventory of property of the debtor within 30 days after qualifying as a trustee, unless such an inventory has already been filed.

DUE DATE	ACTION	CODE §	RULE	EXPLANATION; TIME TO ACT
	Trustee's or debtor in possession's notice of the case to entities holding money or property subject to withdrawal or order of debtor		**2015(a)**	Trustee or debtor in possession must give notice of the case to every entity known to be holding money or property subject to withdrawal or order of debtor, including every bank, savings or building and loan association, public utility company, and landlord with whom debtor has a deposit, and to every insurance company which has issued a policy having a cash surrender value payable to the debtor as soon as possible after commencement of case, except that notice need not be given to any entity who has knowledge or has previously been notified of the case.
	Appointment/election of creditors' committee	**705(a)**	**2003(b)(1)**	At § 341 meeting, qualified creditors may elect a committee of no fewer than 3, and not more than 11 creditors, each of whom holds an allowable unsecured claim.
	Conversion of Chapter 7 case by debtor to Chapter 11 or 13	**706(a)**	**1017(f)(2) 9013**	At any time, if the case has not been converted under §§ 1112 or 1307, upon the motion of the debtor.
	Conversion of case by party in interest to Chapter 11	**706(b)**	**1017(f)(1) 9014**	At any time, upon the filing of a motion and after notice and hearing.
	Conversion of case by debtor to Chapter 12 or 13	**706(c)**	**1017(f) 9013 9014**	A Chapter 7 case may be converted to a Chapter 12 or 13 case only requested by the debtor or the debtor consents.
	New filing periods upon conversion of Chapter 11 or 13 case to Chapter 7		**Interim 1019(2)**	A new time period for filing claims, a complaint objecting to discharge, or a time period for filing a motion under § 707(b) or (c) shall commence under Rules 1017, 3002 or 4004, provided that a new time period shall not commence if a Chapter 7 case had been converted to a Chapter 11, 12, or 13 case and thereafter reconverted to a Chapter 7 case and the time for filing claims, a motion under § 707(b) or (c), or a complaint objecting to discharge or any extension thereof, expired in the original Chapter 7 case. In a case converted to Chapter 7 from Chapter 13, a new period shall commence under Rule 4007 for filing a complaint to obtain a determination that a debt is not dischargeable under § 523(a)(6), unless the case was converted previously to Chapter 13 from Chapter 7 and the time for filing such a complaint expired in the first Chapter 7 case.

DUE DATE	ACTION	CODE §	RULE	EXPLANATION; TIME TO ACT
	Claims filed in superseded cases		1019(3)	All claims actually filed by a creditor in a superseded case are deemed filed in Chapter 7 case.
	Turnover of records and property	521(4)	1019(4)	After qualification or assumption of duties by Chapter 7 trustee, any debtor in possession or trustee previously acting in Chapter 11 or 13 case shall forthwith turn over to Chapter 7 trustee all records and property in possession or control.
	Filing of final report and schedule of postpetition debts after conversion of Chapter 11 case to Chapter 7		1019(5)(A)	Unless otherwise ordered, the debtor in possession or trustee in superseded case: (1) must file a schedule of unpaid debts incurred after commencement of the superseded case, including the name and address of each creditor, within 15 days following entry of order of conversion; and (2) must file and transmit to the U.S. Trustee a final report and account within 30 days following entry of order of conversion.
	Filing of schedule of unpaid postpetition debts and final account in case converted to Chapter 7 from Chapter 13		1019(5)(B)	Unless otherwise ordered, Chapter 13 debtor must file a schedule of unpaid debts incurred after commencement of Chapter 13 case within 15 days following entry of order of conversion. Unless the court orders otherwise, the Chapter 13 trustee shall file and transmit to the U.S. trustee a final report and account within 30 days of the order of conversion.
	Filing of schedule of property acquired postpetition, unpaid postpetition debts and assumed executory contracts and leases if conversion of Chapter 11 or Chapter 13 occurs after plan confirmation		1019(5)(C)	If conversion order is entered after confirmation of a plan, debtor must file a schedule of: (1) property not listed in the final report and account acquired after filing of original petition but before entry of conversion order; (2) unpaid debts not listed in final report and incurred after confirmation but before entry of conversion order; and (3) executory contracts and unexpired leases entered into or assumed after filing of original petition but before entry of conversion order.
	Notice to creditors and filing of schedule of unpaid postpetition, preconversion administrative claims, deadline for filing administrative claims and the deadline for filing claims treated as prepetition claims under § 348(d)		1019(6)	Upon the filing of schedule of unpaid debts pursuant to Rule 1019(5), clerk or other person directed by the court shall give notice to entities listed on schedule of time for filing request for payment of administrative expense and, unless notice of insufficient assets to pay dividend is mailed under Rule 2002(e), the time for filing a claim under § 348(d).

DUE DATE	ACTION	CODE §	RULE	EXPLANATION; TIME TO ACT
	Dismissal of case for cause under § 707(a)	707(a)	1017(a) 1017(d) 9014	Only after notice and hearing and only for cause, including: (1) unreasonable delay of debtor prejudicial to creditors; (2) failure to pay required fees and charges; (3) in a voluntary case, failure of the debtor to file list of creditors and schedules required under § 521(a)(1)[1] within 15 days of petition date or additional time allowed by court. For dismissal of an involuntary petition, see § 303.
	Dismissal for want of prosecution or other cause	707(a)(1)	1017(a)	After hearing on notice as provided in Rule 2002.
	Dismissal for failure to pay filing fee	707(a)(2)	1017(b)(1)	After hearing on notice to debtor and trustee.
	Dismissal of voluntary Chapter 7 or 13 case for failure to file list of creditors and schedules required under § 521(a)(1)	707(a)(3)	1017(c)	Upon motion of the U.S. Trustee, the case may be dismissed for failure of the debtor in a voluntary case to file, within 15 days or such additional time as the court may allow after the filing of the petition, the information required by § 521(a)(1).
	Dismissal (or conversion with the debtor's consent) of Chapter 7 case for abuse by individual debtor whose debts are primarily consumer debts	707(b)	Interim 1017(e)	After notice and a hearing, the court, on its own motion or on a motion by the U.S. Trustee, trustee (or bankruptcy administrator, if any), or any party in interest, may dismiss a case filed by an individual debtor under this chapter whose debts are primarily consumer debts, or, with the debtor's consent, convert such a case to a case under Chapter 11 or 13, if it finds that the granting of relief under Chapter 7 would be an abuse of the provisions of Chapter 7.

[1] It is unclear the scope intended by § 707(a)(3), which still references § 521(1), which only included the list of creditors, schedules and statement of affairs. This section has been replaced by § 521(a)(1), which includes additional filing requirements on the debtor.

DUE DATE	ACTION	CODE §	RULE	EXPLANATION; TIME TO ACT
	Presumption of abuse and "means" test calculation	707(b)(2) 521	**Interim 1007(b)(4)**	In considering under § 707(b)(1) whether the granting of relief would be an abuse, the court shall presume abuse exists if the debtor's current monthly income reduced by the amounts determined under §§ 707(b)(2)(A)(ii), (iii), and (iv), and multiplied by 60 is not less than the lesser of: (1) 25% of the debtor's nonpriority unsecured claims in the case, or $6,000, whichever is greater; or (2) $10,000.
				Unless § 707(b)(2)(D) applies, an individual debtor in a Chapter 7 case with primarily consumer debts shall file a statement of current monthly income prepared as prescribed by the appropriate Official Form, and, if the debtor has current monthly income greater than the applicable median family income for the applicable state and household size, the calculations in accordance with § 707(b), prepared as prescribed by the appropriate Official Form.
				The statement shall be filed with the petition in a voluntary case, or if the petition is accompanied by a list of all the debtor's creditors and their addresses, within 15 days thereafter.
	Notice of presumption of abuse	707(b) 342(d)	**Interim 5008**	In a Chapter 7 case of an individual with primarily consumer debts in which a presumption of abuse has arisen under § 707(b), the clerk shall give to creditors notice of the presumption of abuse in accordance with Rule 2002 within 10 days after the date of the filing of the petition. If the debtor has not filed a statement indicating whether a presumption of abuse has arisen, the clerk shall give notice to creditors within 10 days after the date of the filing of the petition that the debtor has not filed the statement and that further notice will be given if a later filed statement indicates that a presumption of abuse has arisen. If a debtor later files a statement indicating that a presumption of abuse has arisen, the clerk shall give notice to creditors of the presumption of abuse as promptly as practicable.

DUE DATE	ACTION	CODE §	RULE	EXPLANATION; TIME TO ACT
	Restriction on who may file a § 707(b) motion in case of low income debtor	707(b)(6)		Only the judge or U.S. Trustee (or bankruptcy administrator, if any) may file a motion under § 707(b), if the current monthly income of the debtor, or in a joint case, the debtor and the debtor's spouse, as of the date of the order for relief, when multiplied by 12, is equal to or less than: (1) in the case of a debtor in a household of 1 person, the median family income of the applicable State for 1 earner; (2) in the case of a debtor in a household of 2, 3, or 4 individuals, the highest median family income of the applicable State for a family of the same number or fewer individuals; or (3) in the case of a debtor in a household exceeding 4 individuals, the highest median family income of the applicable State for a family of 4 or fewer individuals, plus $525 per month for each individual in excess of 4. For such low income debtors, the judge or U.S. Trustee (or bankruptcy administrator, if any) may not file a motion under § 707(b)(2), using means testing for the presumption of abuse.
	Dismissal for abuse of debtor convicted of crime of violence or drug trafficking crime	707(c)		After notice and a hearing, the court, on a motion by the victim of a crime of violence or a drug trafficking crime, may when it is in the best interest of the victim, dismiss a voluntary case filed under Chapter 7 by a debtor who is an individual if such individual was convicted of such crime.
	Deadline for motion to dismiss for abuse under §§ 707(b) or (c)		**Interim 1017(e)(1)**	A motion to dismiss a case for abuse under §§ 707(b) or (c) may be filed only within 60 days after the first date set for the meeting of creditors under § 341(a), unless, on request filed before the time has expired, the court for cause extends the time for filing the motion to dismiss. The party filing the motion shall set forth in the motion all matters to be considered at the hearing. A motion to dismiss under §§ 707(b)(1) (in which the presumption of abuse arises) and (3) (in which the presumption does not arise) shall state with particularity the circumstances alleged to constitute abuse.

DUE DATE	ACTION	CODE §	RULE	EXPLANATION; TIME TO ACT
	Redemption of tangible personal property which is consumer goods	722 521(a)(6)		An individual debtor may, whether or not the debtor has waived the right to redeem under § 722, redeem tangible personal property intended primarily for personal, family, or household use, from a lien securing a dischargeable consumer debt, if such property is exempted under § 522 or has been abandoned under § 554, by paying the holder of such lien the amount of the allowed secured claim of such holder that is secured by such lien in full at the time of redemption. Under § 521(a)(6), the debtor must surrender possession if the property is not redeemed or a reaffirmation agreement executed within 45 days after the first meeting of creditors.
	Disposition of certain property	725		After commencement of case but before final distribution of property of estate under § 726, after notice and hearing, trustee shall dispose of any property in which an entity other than estate has an interest that has not been disposed of under another section.
	Required notice of proposed abandonment or disposition of property		6007(a)	Trustee or debtor in possession shall give notice of proposed abandonment or disposition of property to U.S. Trustee, all creditors, indenture trustees, and committees; objections must be filed and served within 15 days of mailing of notice, or within time fixed by court; if timely objection is filed, the court may approve the proposed abandonment or disposition only after notice and hearing.
	Payment of dividends to creditors		3009	As promptly as practicable, payable to and mailed to each creditor whose claim has been allowed.
	Time for filing complaint for determination of dischargeability of a debt other than under § 523(c)	523	4007(b) 7001	A complaint may be filed at any time.
	Time for filing complaint for determination of dischargeability of a debt under § 523(c)	523(c)	4007(c) 7001	A complaint seeking to deny a discharge must be filed no later than 60 days following first date set for § 341(a) meeting of creditors; the court must give all creditors not less than 30 days' notice of time so fixed in manner provided by Rule 2002; motions to extend the time to file the complaint must be filed before the expiration of the period and relief granted for cause after notice and hearing.

DUE DATE	ACTION	CODE §	RULE	EXPLANATION; TIME TO ACT
	Time for filing complaint objecting to discharge under § 727(a)	727(a)	4004(a) 7001	A complaint seeking to deny a discharge cannot be filed later than 60 days following first date set for § 341(a) meeting of creditors; no less than 25 days notice of time so fixed shall be given to U.S. Trustee and all creditors as provided in Rules 2002(f) and (k), and to trustee and trustee's attorney.
	Extension of time for filing complaint objecting to discharge		4004(b)	After motion made before time has expired, and after notice and hearing.
	Ground for denial of discharge	727(a)(2)	4004	If debtor, with intent to hinder, delay, or defraud a creditor or an officer of the estate, transferred, removed, destroyed, mutilated, or concealed property of the debtor within 1 year before the petition date or property of the estate after the petition date.
	Ground for denial of discharge	727(a)(3)	4004	If the debtor has concealed, destroyed, mutilated, falsified, or failed to keep or preserve any recorded information, including books, documents, records, and papers, from which the debtor's financial condition or business transactions might be ascertained, unless such act or failure to act was justified under all of the circumstances of the case.
	Ground for denial of discharge	727(a)(4)	4004	If the debtor knowingly and fraudulently, in or in connection with the case: (1) made a false oath or account; (2) presented or used a false claim; (3) gave, offered, received, or attempted to obtain money, property, or advantage, or a promise of money, property, or advantage, for acting or forbearing to act; or (4) withheld from an officer of the estate entitled to possession under this title, any recorded information, including books, documents, records, and papers, relating to the debtor's property or financial affairs.
	Ground for denial of discharge	727(a)(5)	4004	Debtor fails to explain satisfactorily, before determination of denial of discharge under § 727(a), any loss of assets or deficiency of assets.

DUE DATE	ACTION	CODE §	RULE	EXPLANATION; TIME TO ACT
	Ground for denial of discharge	727(a)(6)		If the debtor has refused, in the case: (1) to obey any lawful order of the court, other than an order to respond to a material question or to testify; (2) on the ground of privilege against self-incrimination, to respond to a material question approved by the court or to testify, after the debtor has been granted immunity with respect to the matter concerning which such privilege was invoked; or (3) on a ground other than the properly invoked privilege against self-incrimination, to respond to a material question approved by the court or to testify.
	Ground for denial of discharge	727(a)(7)	4004	If the debtor commits any of acts in §§ 727(a)(2), (3), (4), (5), or (6) on or within 1 year pre-petition or during the case, in connection with another bankruptcy case, concerning an insider.
	Denial of discharge if debtor received discharge in prior Chapter 7 or 11 case	727(a)(8)	4004	Debtor has been granted a discharge under §§ 727 or 1141 in a case commenced within 8 years before the petition date.
	Denial of discharge if debtor received a discharge in prior Chapter 12 or 13 case.	727(a)(9)	4004	Debtor has been granted a discharge under §§ 1228 or 1328 in a case commenced within 6 years before the petition date, unless payments under the plan in such a case totaled amounts set forth in § 727(a)(9).
	Ground for denial of discharge	727(a)(10)	4004(c)	If court approves a written waiver of discharge executed by the debtor after the order for relief. Neither the Code nor the Rules specify any procedure for court approval. Under Rule 4004(c)(1), the discharge may be granted automatically unless the waiver has been filed or one of the other conditions postponing discharge has occurred. See discussion of Rule 4000(c)(1) under "Grant of discharge and notice of discharge order", below.
	Denial of discharge for failure to complete instructional course in personal financial management	727(a)(11) 109(h)(h) 111	Interim 1007(b)(7) and 1007(c)	Discharge denied if debtor failed to complete instructional course in personal financial nonpayment. Unless the U.S. Trustee has determined that the requirement does not apply in the district, an individual debtor shall file a statement regarding completion of a course in personal financial management, prepared as prescribed by the appropriate Official Form, within 45 days after the meeting of creditors under § 341 in a Chapter 7 case.

DUE DATE	ACTION	CODE §	RULE	EXPLANATION; TIME TO ACT
	Denial of discharge for certain defendants in criminal actions or in securities litigation	727(a)(12) 522(q)	4004	If, after notice and a hearing, the court determines that § 522(q)(1) may be applicable to debtor, and a proceeding is pending of the kind described in which the debtor may be found guilty of a felony of the kind described in § 522(q)(1)(A) or found liable for a debt of the kind described in § 522(q)(2), the court shall not grant the debtor a discharge.
	Discharged claims	727(b)	4004	All debts that arose before the date of the order for relief (except as set forth in § 523), and any liability on claim determined under § 502 as if the claim arose before the commencement of the case, whether or not a proof of claim is filed or the claim is allowed under § 502.
	Grant of discharge and notice of discharge order		Interim 4004(c)(1)	On expiration of time fixed for filing complaint objecting to discharge and time fixed for filing motion to dismiss case pursuant to Rule 1017(e), court shall forthwith grant discharge, unless: (1) debtor is not an individual; (2) complaint objecting to discharge has been filed; (3) debtor has filed a waiver under § 727(a)(10); (4) motion to dismiss case under § 707 is pending; (5) motion to extend time for filing objection to discharge is pending; (6) motion to extend time for filing motion to dismiss case under Rule 1017(e) is pending; (7) debtor has not paid the filing fee or other fee; (8) the debtor has not filed the statement regarding completion of a course in personal financial management as required by Rule 1007(b)(7); (9) a motion to delay or postpone discharge under § 727(a)(12) is pending; (10) a presumption that a reaffirmation agreement is an undue hardship has arisen under § 524(m); or (11) a motion to delay discharge, alleging that the debtor has not filed with the court all tax documents required to be filed under § 521(f), is pending.
	Motion for deferral of discharge		4004(c)(2)	Notwithstanding above, on motion of debtor, court may defer entry of discharge order for 30 days and, on motion within such 30-day period, court may defer entry of order to date certain.
	Mailing of copy of order of discharge		4004(g)	Clerk must promptly mail copy of final order of discharge to U.S. Trustee and to all creditors as provided in Rules 2002(f) and (k) and to trustee and trustee's attorney.

DUE DATE	ACTION	CODE §	RULE	EXPLANATION; TIME TO ACT
	Revocation of § 727(a) discharge	727(d)(1), (2) and (3)	7001	On request of the trustee, a creditor, or the U.S. Trustee and after notice and a hearing, the court shall revoke a discharge § 727(a) if: (1) such discharge was obtained through the fraud of the debtor, and the requesting party did not know of such fraud until after the granting of such discharge; (2) the debtor acquired property that is property of the estate, or became entitled to acquire property that would be property of the estate, and knowingly and fraudulently failed to report the acquisition of or entitlement to such property, or to deliver or surrender such property to the trustee; or (3) the debtor committed an act specified in § 727(a)(6) (failure to obey court orders or failure to respond to questions or testify).
	Revocation of discharge for issues related to audits under 28 USC § 586(f)	727(d)(4)	7001	This provision does not take effect until October 20, 2006, when the U.S. Trustee is authorized to contract for random audits to determine the accuracy, veracity, and completeness of petitions, schedules, and other information that the debtor is required to provide. The discharge may be revoked if the debtor fails to satisfactorily explain a material misstatement [revealed] in an audit or failure to make available accounts, papers, documents files and other papers belonging to the debtor and requested for an audit. Neither the statute nor rules contain a deadline to seek revocation of the discharge on these grounds.
	Deadline for request for revocation of discharge	727(e)	7001	Complaint must be filed by trustee, creditor or U.S. Trustee within 1 year after discharge granted if revocation request made under § 727(d)(1) or before the later of 1 year after discharge or date the case is closed if revocation request made under §§ 727(d)(2) or (3).
	Notice of order denying or revoking discharge, or of waiver of discharge		4006	After order becomes final denying or revoking the discharge or a waiver is filed, or, in the case of an individual, if the case is closed without the entry of an order of discharge, the clerk shall promptly give notice to all creditors in accordance with Rule 2002.

Chapter 11, Reorganization, has numerous sections relevant to reorganizations, including railroad reorganizations. Committees, trustees and examiners, conversion and dismissal, collective bargaining agreements, and small business cases are all provided for. Also covered are numerous provisions dealing with plans, including classification of claims and interests, contents, disclosure and solicitation, acceptance, modification and confirmation.

Chapter 11: Reorganization

DUE DATE	ACTION	CODE §	RULE	EXPLANATION; TIME TO ACT
	Substantial consummation of Chapter 11 plan	1101(2)		Time when all of the following are accomplished: transfer of all or substantially all of property proposed by plan to be transferred; assumption by the debtor or successor to the debtor under the plan of the business or management of all or substantially all of property dealt with by plan; and commencement of distribution under the plan.
	Appointment by U.S. Trustee of committee of unsecured creditors and other appropriate committees	1102(a)(1)	2003	Except as provided in § 1102(a)(3) (i.e., after request and for cause in small business case a committee may not be appointed), as soon as practicable after order for relief (note: not applicable to railroad reorganization cases); typically consists of persons holding 7 largest unsecured claims.
	Request of party in interest to appoint additional committee	1102(b)		Upon motion of a party in interest, the court may order appointment of such committees if necessary to assure adequate representation of creditors or equity security holders. The U.S. Trustee appoints any such committee ordered by the court.
	Request of party in interest not to appoint committee in small business case	1102(a)(3)		Upon motion of a party in interest, the court may order that no committee be appointed in a small business case.
	Ordering the U.S. Trustee to change the membership of a committee to ensure adequate representation of creditors or equity security holders	1102(a)(4)		On request of a party in interest and after notice and a hearing, the court may order the United States trustee to change the membership of a committee appointed under § 1104(a), if the court determines that the change is necessary to ensure adequate representation of creditors or equity security holders.
	Duties of committee of creditors to provide access to information and solicit comments	1102(b)(3)		A committee appointed shall: (1) provide access to information for creditors who hold claims of the kind represented by that committee and are not appointed to the committee; (2) solicit and receive comments from such creditors; and (3) be subject to a court order that compels any additional report or disclosure to be made to such creditors.

DUE DATE	ACTION	CODE §	RULE	EXPLANATION; TIME TO ACT
	Motion to review appointment of committee appointed by U.S. Trustee pursuant to § 1102(a)		**2007(a)**	If an official committee consists of the members of a committee organized by creditors pre-petition, then on the motion of a party-in-interest and after notice and hearing, court may determine whether appointment of committee satisfies requirements of § 1102(b)(1).
	Failure to comply with requirements for appointment under § 1102(b)(1)		**2007(c)**	After notice and hearing, court shall direct U.S. Trustee to vacate appointment of committee and may order other appropriate action if court finds that appointment failed to satisfy requirements of § 1102(b)(1).
	Selection and authorization of appointment by committee(s) of attorneys, accountants, or other agents	**1103(a)**	2014	At a scheduled meeting of the committee(s) at which a majority of the members of the committee(s) is present, and with court's approval of appointment(s).
	Meeting between debtor/trustee and committee(s)	**1103(d)**		As soon as practicable after appointment of committee(s).
	Filing of verified Rule 2019 statement by entity or committee representing more than one creditor or equity security holder, except for a committee appointed under §§ 1102 or 1114, and every indenture trustee		**2019**	No time limit set, but should be filed promptly (and any required supplemental statement), because penalty may be court refusal to permit noncomplying party to be heard further or to intervene in the case, and/or invalidation of any authority, acceptance, rejection, or objection given, procured, or received by party that has failed to comply.
	Appointment of trustee or examiner on motion of party in interest	**1104(a)** **1104(c)**	**2007.1**	At any time after commencement of case but before confirmation of a plan, on request of a party in interest or U.S. Trustee and after notice and hearing for causes specified in §§ 1104(a) and (c). Under § 1104(a)(3), a trustee or examiner may be appointed if grounds exist to convert or dismiss the case under § 1112, but the court determines that the appointment of a trustee or an examiner is in the best interests of creditors and the estate.
	Appointment of trustee on motion of the U.S. Trustee	**1104(e)**		The U.S. Trustee, at any time after commencement of case but before confirmation of a plan, is required to seek a trustee if there are reasonable grounds to suspect that current members of the governing body of the debtor, the debtor's chief executive or chief financial officer, or members of the governing body who selected the debtor's chief executive or chief financial officer, participated in actual fraud, dishonesty, or criminal conduct in the management of the debtor or the debtor's public financial reporting. This provision applies to all cases filed on or after April 20, 2005.

DUE DATE	ACTION	CODE §	RULE	EXPLANATION; TIME TO ACT
	Election of trustee after court orders appointment of trustee under § 1104(a)	1104(b)(1)	**2007.1(b)(1)** 2002 2003 2006	Except as provided in § 1163, on request of party in interest made not later than 30 days after court orders appointment of trustee, U.S. Trustee shall convene a meeting of creditors for purpose of electing one disinterested person to serve as trustee. Election of trustee conducted in manner provided in §§ 702(a), (b), and (c).
	Certification if election of trustee undisputed	1104(b)(2)	**Interim 2007.1(b)(3)**	If no dispute arises out of the election, the U.S. Trustee shall promptly file a report certifying the election. The report shall be accompanied by a verified statement of the person elected setting forth the person's connections with the debtor, creditors, any other party in interest, their respective attorneys and accountants, the U.S. Trustee, or any person employed in the office of the U.S. Trustee.
	Report by U.S. Trustee if election of trustee disputed	1104(b)(2)	**Interim 2007.1(b)(3)**	If a dispute arises out of an election, the U.S. Trustee shall promptly file a report stating that the election is disputed, informing the court of the nature of the dispute, and listing the name and address of any candidate elected under any alternative presented by the dispute. The report shall be accompanied by a verified statement of each candidate elected under each alternative presented by the dispute, setting forth the person's connections with the debtor, creditors, any other party in interest, their respective attorneys and accountants, the U.S. Trustee, or any person employed in the office of the U.S. Trustee. Not later than the date on which the report of the disputed election is filed, the U.S. Trustee shall mail a copy of the report and each verified statement to any party in interest that has made a request to convene a meeting under § 1104(b) or to receive a copy of the report, and to any committee appointed under § 1102.

DUE DATE	ACTION	CODE §	RULE	EXPLANATION; TIME TO ACT
	Request for order approving appointment of trustee or examiner		2007.1(c)	An order approving the appointment of a trustee elected an examiner under § 1104(d), shall be made on application of the U.S. Trustee. The application shall state the name of the person appointed and, to the best of the applicant's knowledge, all the person's connections with the debtor, creditors, any other parties in interest, their respective attorneys and accountants, the U.S. Trustee, and persons employed in the office of the U.S. Trustee. The application shall state the names of the parties in interest with whom the U.S. Trustee consulted regarding the appointment. The application shall be accompanied by a verified statement of the person appointed setting forth the person's connections with the debtor, creditors, any other party in interest, their respective attorneys and accountants, the U.S. Trustee, and any person employed in the office of the U.S. Trustee.
			2008	Trustee must notify court and U.S. Trustee of acceptance of office within 5 days after receipt of notice of selection or shall be deemed to have rejected the office.
	Trustee or debtor in possession must file and transmit to U.S. Trustee complete inventory of property of debtor	1106(a) 1107 521	2015(a)	If court directs, within 30 days after qualifying as a trustee or debtor in possession, unless such an inventory has already been filed.
	Trustee or debtor in possession must file and transmit to U.S. Trustee a statement of disbursements made during the calendar quarter and a statement of amount of fee required pursuant to 28 USC § 1930(a)(6) that has been paid for the calendar quarter		2015(a)	On or before the last day of the month after each calendar quarter, until a plan is confirmed or the case is converted or dismissed.

DUE DATE	ACTION	CODE §	RULE	EXPLANATION; TIME TO ACT
	Trustee or debtor in possession must give notice to all entities known to be holding money or property subject to withdrawal or order of the debtor, including every bank, savings or building and loan association, public utility company, and landlord with whom the debtor has a deposit, and to every insurance company which has issued a policy having a cash surrender value payable to the debtor, except that notice need not be given to any entity who has knowledge or has previously been notified of the case		2015(a)	As soon as possible after the case commences.
	Termination of trustee's appointment	1105		At any time before confirmation of a plan, on request of a party in interest or the U.S. Trustee (note: not applicable to railroad reorganization cases) and after notice and hearing.
	Duties of a Chapter 11 trustee	1106(a)(1), (2), and (3)		• perform the duties of a Chapter 7 trustee as specified in §§ 704(2), (5), and (7)–(12) • if the debtor has not done so, file the list schedule, and statements required by § 521(1) • except to the extent that the court orders otherwise, investigate the acts, conduct, assets, liabilities, and financial condition of the debtor, the operation of the debtor's business and the desirability of the continuance of such business, and any other matter relevant to the case or to the formulation of a plan.
	Filing of trustee's statement of investigation conducted under §1106(a)(3)	1106(a)(4)		As soon as practicable, file a statement of any investigation and transmit a copy or a summary to any creditors' committee or equity security holders' committee, to any indenture trustee, and to such other entity as the court designates.
	Chapter 11 Trustee's duty to file a plan, report or recommendation	1106(a)(5)		As soon as practicable, file a plan under§ 1121, file a report of why the trustee will not file a plan, or recommend conversion of the case to a case under Chapter 7, 12, or 13 or dismissal of the case.

DUE DATE	ACTION	CODE §	RULE	EXPLANATION; TIME TO ACT
	Chapter 11 Trustee's duty to furnish information to taxing authority	**1106(a)(6)**		For any year for which the debtor has not filed a tax return required by law, furnish, without personal liability, such information as may be required by the governmental unit with which such tax return was to be filed, in light of the condition of the debtor's books and records and the availability of such information.
	Duty of trustee to provide notice holder of claim for a domestic support obligation and State child support agency	**1106(a)(8) and (c)**		If there is a claim for a domestic support obligation, the trustee shall: (1) provide written notice to the holder of the claim of such claim and of the right of such holder to use the services of the State child support enforcement agency for assistance in collecting child support during and after the case; (2) include in the notice the address and telephone number of such State child support enforcement agency; and (3) include in the notice an explanation of the rights of such holder to payment of such claim under Chapter 7.

The trustee shall also provide written notice to such State child support enforcement agency of such claim; and include in the notice the name, address, and telephone number of the holder of the claim.

At such time as the debtor is granted a discharge, the trustee shall provide written notice to the holder and to the State child support enforcement agency of : (1) the granting of the discharge; (2) the last recent known address of the debtor; (3) the last recent known name and address of the debtor's employer; and (4) the name of each creditor that holds a claim that is not discharged under § 523(a)(2), (4), or (14A) of or was reaffirmed by the debtor under § 524(c). |

DUE DATE	ACTION	CODE §	RULE	EXPLANATION; TIME TO ACT
	Right of secured party with a security interest in, or a lessor or conditional vendor of, aircraft equipment described in § 1110(a)(2), to take possession of such equipment, in compliance with a security agreement, lease, or conditional sale contract	**1110(a)** **1110(b)**		Not affected by § 362, or the power of any court to enjoin the taking of possession, unless: (a) within 60 days from order for relief, and after court approval, trustee agrees to perform all obligations that become due on or after the date of the order under such security agreement, lease, or, conditional sale contract; and (b) any default (except § 365(b)(2) default) under such security agreement, lease, or conditional sale contract that occurs before the date of the order is cured before the expiration of the 60-day period and that occurs after the date of the order is cured before the later of 30 days after the default or expiration of 60-day period. Subject to approval of the court, the parties may agree to extend the 60 day period.
	Duty to surrender and return aircraft equipment described in § 1110(a)	**1110(c)**		The trustee shall immediately surrender and return equipment to secured party, lessor or conditional vendor entitled to possession under § 1110(a)(1) upon written demand.
	Proofs of claim or interest deemed filed under § 501 in Chapter 9 and 11 cases	**1111(a)** **501**	**3003(b)** **and (c)(2)**	For any claim or interest that appears in the schedules filed under §§ 521(1) or 1106(a)(2), except claims or interests scheduled as disputed, contingent, or unliquidated.
	Election of application of § 1111(b)(2) by class of secured creditors	**1111(b)(2)**	**3014**	May be made at any time prior to conclusion of disclosure statement hearing, or within later time fixed by court.
	Conversion to Chapter 7 by debtor	**1112(a)**	**1017(f)(2)** **9013**	At any time by debtor, upon motion by the debtor, filed and served in accordance with Rule 9013, if § 1112(a) exceptions do not exist: • debtor is not a debtor in possession • case was commenced as an involuntary Chapter 11 • case was converted to Chapter 11 on request of party other than debtor.

DUE DATE	ACTION	CODE §	RULE	EXPLANATION; TIME TO ACT
	Conversion to Chapter 7 or dismissal of case on request of party in interest	**1112(b)(1)** **1112(b)(4)**	**1017(f)(1)** **1017(a)** 9014	Except as provided in §§ 1102(b)(2), (c) 1104(a)(3), on motion of a party in interest, and after notice and a hearing, absent unusual circumstances specifically identified by the court that establish that the requested conversion or dismissal is not in the best interests of creditors and the estate, the court shall convert a case under this chapter to a case under Chapter 7 or may dismiss a case under this chapter, whichever is in the best interests of creditors and the estate, if the movant establishes cause, including: • substantial or continuing loss to or diminution of the estate and the absence of a reasonable likelihood of rehabilitation; • gross mismanagement of the estate; • failure to maintain appropriate insurance that poses a risk to the estate or to the public; • unauthorized use of cash collateral substantially harmful to 1 or more creditors; • failure to comply with an order of the court; • unexcused failure to satisfy timely filing or reporting requirements under the Code or Rules; • failure to attend the meeting of creditors or an examination ordered under Rule 2004; • failure to timely provide information or attend meetings reasonably requested by the U.S. Trustee (or the bankruptcy administrator); • failure to timely pay taxes owed after the date of the order for relief or to file tax returns due after the date of the order for relief; • failure to file a disclosure statement, or to file or confirm a plan, within the time fixed by the Code or court order; • failure to pay any fees or charges required under Chapter 123 of title 28 (including bankruptcy fees under 28 USC§ 1930); • revocation of an order of confirmation under § 1144; • inability to effectuate substantial consummation of a confirmed plan; • material default by the debtor with respect to a • confirmed plan; • termination of a confirmed plan by reason of the occurrence of a condition specified in the plan; and • failure of the debtor to pay any domestic support obligation that first becomes payable after the date of the filing of the petition.

DUE DATE	ACTION	CODE §	RULE	EXPLANATION; TIME TO ACT
	No conversion or dismissal under specified circumstances	1112(b)(2)		Conversion or dismissal shall not be granted absent unusual circumstances specifically identified by the court that establish that such relief is [not][1] in the best interests of creditors and the estate, if the debtor or another party in interest objects and establishes that: (1) in the case of a small business debtor there is a reasonable likelihood that a plan will be confirmed within the timeframes established in §§ 1121(e) and 1129(e), or for any other debtor, within a reasonable period of time; and (2) the grounds for granting such relief include an act or omission of the debtor, other than under § 1112(b)(4)(A) (substantial or continuing loss or diminution of the estate), for which there exists a reasonable justification and that will be cured within a reasonable period of time fixed by the court.
	Deadlines for the court to hold hearing on motion to convert	1112(b)(3)	1017(f)(1)	The court shall commence the hearing on a motion under § 1112(b) not later than 30 days after filing of the motion, and shall decide the motion not later than 15 days after commencement of such hearing, unless the movant expressly consents to a continuance for a specific period of time or compelling circumstances prevent the court from meeting the time limits.
	Conversion to Chapter 12 or 13 by debtor	1112(d)	1017(a) 1017(f)(1)	Only upon motion of the debtor, after notice and a hearing, if the debtor has not been discharged under § 1141(d) and such relief is equitable.
	Conversion to Chapter 7 or dismissal on motion of U.S. Trustee for failure to file information required under § 521(a)(1)[2]	1112(e)	1017(c)	Except as provided in § 1121(c) and (f), on motion of the U.S. Trustee, after a hearing upon notice to the debtor and trustee, if the debtor in a voluntary case fails to file information required by § 521[a] (1) within 15 days after petition or such longer time as court allows.
	Notice of dismissal for failure to pay filing fee	1112(e)	1017(b)	After hearing on notice to debtor and trustee, the court may dismiss the case.

[1] The authors have concluded that the bracketed "not," contained in the statute, was an error, and that the moving party must establish unusual circumstances justifying conversion or dismissal if the debtor establishes the elements of §1112(b)(2)(A) and (B).

[2] The amendment to § 1112(e) did not account for the renumbering in § 521. Former § 521(1) is now § 521(a)(1).

DUE DATE	ACTION	CODE §	RULE	EXPLANATION; TIME TO ACT
	Assumption or rejection of collective bargaining agreements by debtor	1113(a), (b), and (c)		Only if requirements of § 1113 are met. Application for rejection can only be made if trustee or debtor in possession, subsequent to petition date but prior to filing application to reject, has made a reasonable proposal to the authorized representatives, based on the most complete and reliable information available at the time of such proposal, which provides for those necessary modifications in the employee benefits and protection that are necessary to permit the reorganization of the debtor and assures that all creditors, the debtor and all of the affected parties are treated fairly and equitably; and provide, subject to § 1113(d)(3), the representative of the employees with such relevant information as is necessary to evaluate the proposal. From the time the proposal is made until the date of the hearing, the trustee or debtor in possession shall meet, at reasonable times with the authorized representative to confer in good faith to reach agreement on modifications. The court will approve rejection only if: (1) the proposal fulfills these requirements; (2) the employees refused to accept without good cause; and (3) the balance of the equities demand clearly favors rejection of such agreement.
	Hearing on motion to reject collective bargaining agreement	1113(d)(1)		Upon filing of application for rejection, court must schedule hearing within 14 days, and adequate notice must be given to all interested parties at least 10 days prior to hearing; court may extend time for commencement of hearing up to an additional 7 days or such additional time as trustee (or debtor in possession) and the employees' representative(s) agree.
	Ruling on motion to reject collective bargaining agreement	1113(d)(2)		Court must rule within 30 days from commencement of hearing; court may extend time for ruling for such additional time as trustee and employees' representative(s) agree. If court fails to timely rule, trustee or debtor in possession may terminate or alter any provisions of the collective bargaining agreement pending the ruling of the court.

DUE DATE	ACTION	CODE §	RULE	EXPLANATION; TIME TO ACT
	Court authorization of interim changes in terms, conditions, wages, benefits, or work rules provided by collective bargaining agreement	1113(e)		After notice and hearing; if during period when collective bargaining agreement continues in effect, and if essential to continuation of debtor's business, or in order to avoid irreparable damage to estate. Hearing shall be scheduled in accordance with the needs of the trustee or debtor in possession.
	Appointment of committee of retired employees to serve as authorized representative of persons receiving "retiree benefits" as defined in § 1114(a) covered by collective bargaining agreement when labor organizaton elects not to act in such capacity or when different representation is appropriate	1114(c)(1) 1114(c)(2) 1114(d)		If the trustee or debtor in possession seeks to modify or not pay retiree benefits and the retiree benefits are covered by a collective bargaining agreement, the court shall, upon a motion of a party in interest, and after notice and a hearing, order the appointment of a committee of retired employees if: (a) the labor organization elects not to act as the authorized representative; or (2) the court determines that different representation is appropriate. The U.S. Trustee shall appoint the members of such committee.
	Appointment of committee of retired employees to serve as authorized representative of persons receiving retiree benefits not covered by collective bargaining agreement	1114(c)(2) 1114(d)		If the trustee or debtor in possession seeks to modify or not pay retiree benefits which are not covered by a collective bargaining agreement, upon motion of a party in interest and after notice and a hearing, the court shall appoint a committee of retired employees to serve as an authorized representative of persons receiving retiree benefits. The U.S. Trustee shall appoint the members of such committee.
	Payment of retiree benefits to retired employees	1114(e)(1)		Debtor in possession or trustee shall timely pay and shall not modify retiree benefits without either the agreement of the authorized representative of the retired employees, in which case the debtor must pay the retiree benefits as agreed, or after court order, upon motion of the debtor, and after notice and a hearing or agreement of parties, after notice and hearing, in compliance with the provisions of §§ 1114(g) and (h).

DUE DATE	ACTION	CODE §	RULE	EXPLANATION; TIME TO ACT
	Requirement of the debtor to make proposal prior to application for entry of order by the court modifying retiree benefit payments	1114(f) 1114(g)		Prior to filing application to modify retiree benefits, the debtor must make a reasonable proposal to authorized representative of the retirees based on the most complete and reliable information available at the time of such proposal, which provides for those necessary modifications in the retiree benefits that are necessary to permit the reorganization of the debtor and assures that all creditors, the debtor and all of the affected parties are treated fairly and equitably; and provide, subject to § 1114(k)(3), the representative of the retirees with such relevant information as is necessary to evaluate the proposal.

From the time the proposal is made until the date of the hearing, the trustee or debtor in possession shall meet, at reasonable times with the authorized representative to confer in good faith to reach agreement on modifications.

The court will approve modifications only if: (1) the proposal fulfills these requirements; (2) the employees refused to accept without good cause; and (3) the modification is necessary to permit the reorganization of the debtor and assures that all creditors, the debtor, and all affected parties are treated fairly and equitably, and is clearly favored by the balance of the equities. |
| | Court authorization to implement interim modifications in retiree benefits prior to court issuing final order | 1114(h) | | After notice and hearing, if essential to the continuation of the debtor's business, or in order to avoid irreparable damage to the estate.

Hearing shall be scheduled in accordance with the needs of the trustee or debtor in possession. |
| | Hearing on application to modify retiree benefits | 1114(k)(1) | | Upon filing of application for modification, court must schedule hearing within 14 days, and adequate notice must be given to all interested parties at least 10 days prior to hearing; court may extend time for commencement of hearing up to an additional 7 days or such additional time as all parties agree. |
| | Ruling on application to modify retiree benefits | 1114(k)(2) | | Court must rule within 90 days from commencement of hearing; court may extend time for ruling for such additional time as all parties agree. If court fails to timely rule, debtor may implement modified retiree benefits pending the ruling of the court. |

DUE DATE	ACTION	CODE §	RULE	EXPLANATION; TIME TO ACT
	Modification of retirement benefits while debtor was insolvent during the 180-day period prior to the petition date	1114(l)		On motion of party in interest, and after notice and a hearing, court may reinstate as of the date modification was made such benefits, unless court finds that balance of equities clearly favors such modification.
	Additional property of the estate in Chapter 11 case of an individual	1115		In addition to the property specified in § 541, property of the estate includes: (1) all property of the kind specified in § 541 that the debtor acquires after the commencement of the case but before the case is closed, dismissed, or converted to a case under Chapter 7, 12, or 13, whichever occurs first; and (2) earnings from services performed by the debtor after the commencement of the case but before the case is closed, dismissed, or converted to a case under Chapter 7, 12, or 13, whichever occurs first.
	Additional duties of trustee or debtor in possession in small business Chapter 11 case— financial documents and tax returns	1116(1)		In a small business case, the trustee or debtor in possession shall append to voluntary petition, or in involuntary case, file not later than 7 days after the order of relief, the small business debtors most recent balance sheet, statement of operations, cash-flow statement, and Federal income tax return; or a statement under penalty of perjury that no such documents have been prepared or filed.
	Additional duties of trustee or debtor in possession in small business Chapter 11 case— attendance at meetings	1116(2)		In a small business case, the trustee or debtor in possession shall attend through its senior management and personnel and counsel, meetings scheduled by the court or U.S. Trustee, including initial debtor interviews, scheduling conferences, and meetings scheduled under § 341, unless the court, after notice and a hearing, waives such requirement upon a finding of extraordinary and compelling circumstances.
	Duty of the U.S. Trustee in small business Chapter 11 case	28 USC 586		In each of such small business cases, the U.S. Trustee shall conduct an initial debtor interview as soon as practicable after the date of the order for relief but before the first meeting scheduled under § 341(a), at which time the U.S. Trustee shall perform the actions required under 28 USC § 586(a)(7).
	Duty to timely file schedules and statements in small business Chapter 11 case	1116(3)	Interim 9006(b)(3)	In a small business case, the trustee or debtor in possession shall timely file schedules and statements of financial affairs, unless the court, after notice and a hearing, grants an extension, which shall not extend such time period to a date later than 30 days after the order for relief, absent extraordinary and compelling circumstances.

DUE DATE	ACTION	CODE §	RULE	EXPLANATION; TIME TO ACT
	The debtor may file a plan	1121(a)		Plan may be filed by the debtor with the petition or at any time during the case.
	Debtor's exclusive right to file a plan	1121(b)	3016	Within 120 days from order for relief ("exclusivity period"), except as provided in § 1121, only the debtor may file a plan.
	Right of any party in interest to file a plan	1121(c)	3016	The non-exclusive right of any party in interest (including the debtor, trustee, committee, creditor, equity security holder or indenture trustee) to file a plan is available only if a trustee has been appointed, the exclusive period has expired, or the debtor has not filed a plan that is accepted by each impaired class before 180 days after order for relief.
	Request for extension or reduction of exclusivity and/or solicitation periods	1121(d)(1) 1121(d)(2)(A) 1121(d)(2)(B)		On motion made by party in interest within applicable period and after notice and hearing, for cause, the court may extend or reduce the 120 day exclusivity period of § 1121(b) or the 180 day period specified in § 1121(c)(3) (the "solicitation period"). The exclusive period may not be extended beyond the date that is 18 months after date of order for relief under Chapter 11. The solicitation period may not be extended beyond the date that is 20 months after date of order for relief under Chapter 11.
	Exclusivity period in small business cases	1121(e)(1)	3016	Only debtor may file plan for first 180 days after order for relief, unless that period is extended, after notice and a hearing; or court, for cause, orders otherwise.
	Deadlines for filing plan and disclosure statement (if any) in small business cases	1121(e)(2)		Not later than 300 days after the order for relief.
	Extensions in small business cases of exclusivity period, deadlines for filing plan and disclosure statement (if any), and deadline of § 1129(e) requiring court to confirm plan complying with the Code within 45 days of filing of plan	1121(e)(3)		The deadlines under § 1121(e) and the deadline for confirmation in § 1129(e) may be extended only if, debtor, after providing notice to parties in interest, demonstrates by a preponderance of evidence that it is more likely than not that a plan will be confirmed within reasonable time, a new deadline is imposed at the time extension is granted, and order extending time is signed before the existing deadline expires.
	Requirement for filing disclosure statement in cases other than small business cases		Interim 3016(b)	A disclosure statement shall be filed with the plan or within a time fixed by the court.

DUE DATE	ACTION	CODE §	RULE	EXPLANATION; TIME TO ACT
	Classification of claims and interests	1122	3013	The plan may provide for classification of claims or interests or on motion of a party in interest, after notice and a hearing, the court may determine the classification of claims and interests.
	Limitations on post-petition solicitation	1125(a) 1125(b)	3017	Acceptance or rejection of plan may not be solicited after commencement of case from holder of claim or interest unless, at the time of or before the solicitation, the plan or a summary thereof and a written disclosure statement, approved by court as containing adequate information after notice and hearing, is transmitted to such holder.
	Authorization of pre-petition disclosure	1125(g)		Notwithstanding § 1125(b), acceptance or rejection of plan may be solicited if such solicitation complies with applicable nonbankruptcy law and if such holder was solicited before the commencement of the case in a manner complying with applicable nonbankruptcy law.
	Filing a disclosure statement	1125	3016(b)	Filed with plan or within a time fixed by court.
	Hearing on disclosure statement and objections thereto	1125(b)	3017(a)	Court must hold hearing on no less than 25 days notice to debtor, creditors, equity holders, U.S. Trustee, and other parties in interest as provided in Rule 2002. Plan and disclosure statement must be mailed only to the debtor, the trustee, any official committees, the SEC, and any party who requests a copy. Parties receiving the notice of hearing may request a copy. Objections to disclosure statement must be filed and served on debtor, trustee, committees, U.S. Trustee, and others designated by court, at any time prior to approval of the disclosure statement or by such earlier date as the court may fix (requirements for service of objections and the deadline are customarily contained in the notice of hearing).
	Dates fixed for voting on plan and confirmation		3017(c)	On or before approval of disclosure statement, court must fix a time within which holders of claims and interests may accept or reject the plan and may fix a date for confirmation hearing.

DUE DATE	ACTION	CODE §	RULE	EXPLANATION; TIME TO ACT
	Transmission by debtor in possession, trustee, proponent of plan, or clerk of plan disclosure statement, notice of confirmation hearing and objection deadlines		3017(d)	Upon approval of a disclosure statement, except to the extent that the court orders otherwise with respect to one or more unimpaired classes of creditors or equity security holders, the debtor in possession, trustee, proponent of the plan, or clerk of the court orders shall mail to all creditors and equity security holders, and in a Chapter 11 reorganization case shall transmit to the U.S. Trustee: (1) the plan or a court-approved summary of the plan; (2) the disclosure statement approved by the court; (3) notice of the time within which acceptances and rejections of the plan may be filed; and (4) any other information as the court may direct. In addition, notice of the time fixed for filing objections and the hearing on confirmation shall be mailed to all creditors and equity security holders in accordance with Rule 2002(b), and a form of ballot conforming to the appropriate Official Form shall be mailed to creditors and equity security holders entitled to vote on the plan. If the court opinion approving the disclosure statement is not transmitted or only a summary of the plan is transmitted, the court opinion or the plan shall be provided on request of a party in interest at the plan proponent's expense. If the court orders that the disclosure statement and the plan or a summary of the plan shall not be mailed to any unimpaired class, notice that the class is designated in the plan as unimpaired and notice of the name and address of the person from whom the plan or summary of the plan and disclosure statement may be obtained upon request and at the plan proponent's expense, shall be mailed to members of the unimpaired class together with the notice of the time fixed for filing objections to and the hearing on confirmation. For the purposes of Rule 3017(d), creditors and equity security holders shall include holders of securities of record on the date the order approving the disclosure statement is entered or another date fixed by the court, for cause, after notice and a hearing.

DUE DATE	ACTION	CODE §	RULE	EXPLANATION; TIME TO ACT
	Transmission to beneficial holders of securities of Rule 3017(d) documents		3017(e)	At disclosure statement hearing, court must consider the procedures for transmitting documents and information required by Rule 3017(d) to beneficial holders of securities and determine the adequacy of those procedures and enter an appropriate order.
	Notice and transmission of documents to entities subject to an injunction under a plan		3017(f)	If a plan provides for an injunction against conduct not otherwise enjoined under the Code and an entity that would be subject to the injunction is not a creditor or equity security holder, at the hearing held under Rule 3017(a), the court shall consider procedures for providing the entity with: (1) at least 25 days notice of the time fixed for filing objections and the hearing on confirmation of the plan containing the information described in Rule 2002(c)(3); and (2) to the extent feasible, a copy of the plan and disclosure statement.
	Plan may contain information eliminating need for separate disclosure statement	1125(f)(1)	Interim 3016(b)	Notwithstanding § 1125(b), in small business case, the court may determine that the plan itself provides adequate information and that a separate disclosure statement is not necessary. If the plan is intended to provide adequate information under § 1125(f)(1), Rule 3017.1 shall apply as if the plan is a disclosure statement.
	Official or standard form disclosure statement in small business case	1125(f)(2)		Notwithstanding § 1125(b), in small business case, the court may approve a disclosure statement submitted on standard forms or that substantially conform to an official form approved under 28 USC § 2075 or other standard form approved by the court.

DUE DATE	ACTION	CODE §	RULE	EXPLANATION; TIME TO ACT
	Conditional approval of disclosure statement in small business case	1125(f)(3)	3017.1	Notwithstanding § 1125(b), in small business case, plan acceptances and rejections may be solicited based on conditionally approved disclosure statement. Such conditionally approved disclosure statement must be mailed not later than 25 days before confirmation hearing. The hearing on disclosure statement may be combined with confirmation hearing; hearing held on no less than 25 days notice. Conditional approval may be sought by application of the plan proponent or as a result of action by the court on its own initiative. On or before conditionally approving a disclosure statement in a small business case court shall: (1) fix a time for holders of claims and interests to accept or reject the plan; (2) fix a time for filing objections to the disclosure statement; (3) fix a date for a hearing to be held to consider final approval of the disclosure statement in the event that an objection is filed; and (4) fix a date for the hearing to consider confirmation of the plan. Rules 3017(a), (b), (c), and (e) do not apply to a conditionally approved disclosure statement. Rule 3017(d) applies to a conditionally approved disclosure statement, except that conditional approval is considered approval of the disclosure statement for the purpose of applying Rule 3017(d).
	Final approval of disclosure statement in small business case		3017.1(c)	Notice of the time for filing objections to final approval shall be given in accordance with Rule 2002 and may be combined with hearing on notice of confirmation of the plan. Objections to the disclosure statement shall be filed, transmitted to the U.S. Trustee, and served on the debtor, the trustee, any committee appointed under the Code and any other entity designated by the court at any time before final approval of the disclosure statement or by an earlier date as the court may fix. If a timely objection to the disclosure is filed, the court shall hold a hearing to consider final approval before or combined with the hearing on confirmation of the plan.

DUE DATE	ACTION	CODE §	RULE	EXPLANATION; TIME TO ACT
	Entities entitled to accept or reject plan; time for acceptance or rejection	1126(a)	3018(a) 3018(c)	A holder of an allowed claim or interest may accept or reject plan; plan may be accepted or rejected within time fixed by court pursuant to Rule 3017. An acceptance or rejection shall be in writing, identify the plan or plans accepted or rejected and be signed by creditor or equity security holder or authorized agent. Subject to Rule 3018(b), equity holder or creditor whose claim is based on security of record is not entitled to accept or reject a plan unless they are a holder of record on the date the order approving the disclosure statement is entered.
	Temporary allowance of claim or interest for purposes of voting on plan	1126(a) 502(c)	3018(a)	Notwithstanding an objection to a claim or interest, the court, after notice and hearing, may temporarily allow the claim or interest in an amount the court deems proper for purposes of voting to accept or reject the plan.
	Change or withdrawal of acceptance or rejection of plan	1126	3018(a)	For cause shown, after notice and hearing, the court may permit a creditor or equity security holder to change or withdraw an acceptance or rejection of the plan.
	Pre-petition acceptance or rejections deemed accepted or rejected postpetition	1126(b)	3018(b)	Equity holder or creditor whose claim is based on security of record who accepted or rejected the plan before the commencement of the case shall not be deemed to have accepted or rejected pursuant to § 1126(b) unless they were a holder of record on the date specified in the pre-petition solicitation. Holder of claim or interest who accepted or rejected plan before commencement of case shall not be deemed to have accepted or rejected plan if court finds, after notice and hearing, that plan was not transmitted to substantially all creditors and equity holders of same class, that an unreasonably short time was prescribed to accept or reject plan, or solicitation was not in compliance with § 1126(b).
	Voting requirement for acceptance by a class of creditors	1126(c)		A class of claims has accepted a plan if such plan has been accepted by creditors, other than any entity designated under § 1127(e), that hold at least two thirds in amount and more than one-half in number of the allowed claims of such class held by creditors, other than any entity designated under § 1127(e), that have accepted or rejected such plan.

DUE DATE	ACTION	CODE §	RULE	EXPLANATION; TIME TO ACT
	Voting requirement for acceptance by a class of interests	1126(d)		A class of interests has accepted a plan if such plan has been accepted by holders of such interests, other than any entity designated under § 1127(e), that hold at least two-thirds in amount of the allowed interests of such class held by holders of such interests, other than any entity designated under designated under § 1127(e), that have accepted or rejected such plan.
	Designation by court of entity whose acceptance or rejection of plan was not in good faith, or was not solicited or procured in good faith or in accordance with Title 11	1126(e)		On request of a party in interest, and after notice and a hearing the court may designate an entity whose acceptance of rejection of a plan was not in good faith, or was not solicited or procured in good faith or in accordance with Title 11. Such acceptances or rejections shall not be considered to determine acceptance or rejection of each class under § 1126(d).
	Modification of plan by proponent of plan before confirmation	1127(a) 1127(c) 1127(f)	**Interim 3019(a)**	The proponent of a plan may modify such plan at any time before confirmation, but may not modify such plan so that such plan as modified fails to meet the requirements of §§ 1122 and 1123. After the proponent of a plan files a modification of such plan with the court, the plan as modified becomes the plan, but only after there has been disclosure under § 1125 as the court may direct, notice and a hearing, and such modification is approved. §§ 1121 through 1128 and the requirements of § 1129 apply to any modification.
	Deemed acceptances or rejections of modified plan by creditors on interest holders who do not change its vote	1127(d)		Any holder of a claim or interest that has accepted or rejected a plan is deemed to have accepted or rejected, as the case may be, such plan as modified, unless, within the time fixed by the court, such holder changes such holder's previous acceptance or rejection.
	Deemed acceptances of modified plan before confirmation by previously accepting creditors not adversely affected		**Interim 3019(a)**	If the court finds after hearing on notice to the trustee, any committee appointed under the Code, and any other entity designated by the court that the proposed modification does not adversely change the treatment of the claim of any creditor or the interest of any equity security holder who has not accepted in writing the modification, it shall be deemed accepted by all creditors and equity security holders who have previously accepted the plan.

DUE DATE	ACTION	CODE §	RULE	EXPLANATION; TIME TO ACT
	Modification of plan after confirmation	**1127(b) and (c)**		The proponent of the plan or the reorganized debtor may modify the plan at any time after confirmation and before substantial consummation, but may not modify such plan so that such plan as modified fails to meet the requirements of §§ 1122 and 1123. Such plan as modified becomes the plan only if circumstances warrant such modification and the court, after notice and a hearing, confirms such plan as modified, under § 1129. The proponent of a modification must meet the disclosure requirements of § 1125 with respect to the plan as modified.
	Modification of confirmed plan in individual Chapter 11 case before completion of payments	**1127(e)**	**Interim 3019(b)**	If the debtor is an individual, the plan may be modified at anytime after confirmation but before completion of payments under plan, upon request of debtor, trustee, U.S. Trustee, or holder of allowed unsecured claim to: (1) increase or reduce payments under plan; (2) extend or reduce time for such payments; or (3) alter amount of distribution to a particular creditor to account for payments made to such creditor outside of plan. Any objection to the proposed modification shall be filed and served on the debtor, the trustee, and any other entity designated by the court, and shall be transmitted to the United States trustee.
			Interim 3019(b) 9014	A request to modify the plan under § 1127(e) shall identify the proponent and shall be filed together with the proposed modification. The clerk, or some other person as the court may direct, shall give the debtor, the trustee, and all creditors not less than 20 days notice by mail of the time fixed for filing objections and, if an objection is filed, the hearing to consider the proposed modification, unless the court orders otherwise with respect to creditors who are not affected by the proposed modification. A copy of the notice shall be transmitted to the United States trustee. A copy of the proposed modification shall be included with the notice. Any objection to the proposed modification shall be filed and served on the debtor, the proponent of the modification, the trustee, and any other entity designated by the court, and shall be transmitted to the United States trustee. An objection to a proposed modification is governed by Rule 9014.

DUE DATE	ACTION	CODE §	RULE	EXPLANATION; TIME TO ACT
	Deposit with trustee or debtor in possession of consideration required by plan to be distributed on confirmation		**3020(a)**	Court may order prior to confirmation order.
	Objections to confirmation of plan	**1128(b)**	**3020(b)(1)**	Must be filed and served on debtor, trustee, proponent of plan, committees, U.S. Trustee, and any other entity designated by court, within time fixed by court.
	Plan confirmation hearing	**1129(a)** **1129(b)** 1128(a)	**3020(b)(2)** 9014	After notice and hearing provided for in Rule 2002 and if the court determines that all the requirements of § 1129(a) have been met, the court may confirm the plan. If no objection has been timely filed, the court may determine that the plan has been proposed in good faith and not by any means prohibited by law without receiving evidence of these issues. If not every class of claims or interests has accepted the plan (§ 1129(a)(8)), but every other requirement under § 1129(a) are met, the court may confirm the plan notwithstanding the rejection by one or more classes ("cramdown") under § 1129(b), if the plan does not discriminate unfairly and is fair and equitable with respect to each impaired class that has not accepted, including the applicable fair and equitable standards under § 1129(b)(2).
	Payment of administrative expense claims and "gap" claims	**1129(a)(9)(B)**		The court shall confirm the plan only if, with respect to a claim of a kind specified in §§ 507(a)(2) or (3), on the effective date of the plan, the holder of such claim will receive on account of such claim cash equal to the allowed amount of such claim.
	Payment of priority claims under plan for domestic support obligation and the priority claims or wages, salaries, commissions, employee benefits, grain producers and fishermen	**1129(a)(9)(B)**		The court shall confirm the plan only if, with respect to a class of claims of a kind specified in §§ 507(a)(1), (4), (5), (6), or (7), each holder of a claim of such class will receive if such class has accepted the plan, deferred cash payments of a value, as of the effective date of the plan, equal to the allowed amount of such claim; or if such class has not accepted the plan, cash on the effective date of the plan equal to the allowed amount of such claim.

DUE DATE	ACTION	CODE §	RULE	EXPLANATION; TIME TO ACT
	Payment of priority and secured tax claims under plan	1129(a)(9)(C) and (D)		The court shall confirm the plan only if, with respect to a claim of a kind specified in § 507(a)(8) and with respect to a secured claim which would otherwise meet the description of an unsecured claim of a governmental unit under § 507(a)(8) but for the secured status of that claim, the holder of such claim must receive on account of such claim regular installment payments in cash of a total value, as of the effective date of the plan, equal to the allowed amount of such claim over a period ending not later than 5 years after the date of the order for relief in a manner not less favorable than the most favored non-priority unsecured claim provided for by the plan (other than cash payments made to a convenience class of creditors under § 1122(b)).
	Condition to confirmation of plan in case of individual—payment of domestic support obligations	1129(a)(14)		The court shall confirm the plan only if an individual debtor required by a judicial or administrative order, or by statute, to pay a domestic support obligation has paid all amounts payable under such order or such statute for such obligation that first became payable after the date of the filing of the petition.
	Condition to confirmation of plan in case of individual over objection of unsecured creditor—projected disposable income	1129(a)(15)		In a case in which the debtor is an individual and in which the holder of an allowed unsecured claim objects to the confirmation of the plan, the court shall confirm the plan only if: (1) the value, as of the effective date of the plan, of the property to be distributed under the plan on account of such claim is not less than the amount of such claim (full payment); or (2) the value of the property to be distributed under the plan is not less than the projected disposable income of the debtor (as defined in § 1325(b)(2)) to be received during the 5-year period beginning on the date that the first payment is due under the plan, or during the period for which the plan provides payments, whichever is longer.
	Condition to confirmation of plan in case of an individual—filing of requested tax returns	1129 521(f)		Section 1228(b) of BAPCPA provides that "[t]he court shall not confirm a plan of reorganization in the case of an individual under Chapter 11 . . . unless requested tax documents have been filed with the court." This section was not designated as an amendment to any Code provision, but is nonetheless a requirement of confirmation.

DUE DATE	ACTION	CODE §	RULE	EXPLANATION; TIME TO ACT
	Deadline for confirmation in small business case			In a small business case, the court shall confirm a plan that complies with the applicable provisions of the Code that is filed in accordance with § 1121(e) not later than 45 days after the plan is filed unless the time for confirmation is extended in accordance with § 1121(e)(3).
	Form of order confirming plan, including content of supplemental injunction		3020(c)(1)	The order shall conform to the Official Form No. 15. If the plan provides for an injunction against conduct not otherwise enjoined under the Code, the order shall : • describe in reasonable detail all acts enjoined; • be specific in its terms regarding the injunction; and • identify the entities subject to the injunction.
	Notice of entry order confirming plan (including entities subject to supplemental injunction)		3020(c)(2) and (3)	Notice of entry of the order of confirmation shall be mailed promptly to the debtor, the trustee, creditors, equity security holders, other parties in interest, and, if known, to any identified entity subject to an injunction provided for in the plan against conduct not otherwise enjoined under the Code, and transmitted to the U.S. Trustee.
	Stay of confirmation order		3020(e)	An order confirming a plan is stayed until the expiration of 10 days after the entry of the order, unless the court orders otherwise.
	Effect of confirmation—Discharge	1141(a)		Except as otherwise provided in the plan or the order confirming the plan, confirmation of the plan discharges the debtor from any debt which arose before the date of confirmation and any debt of a kind specified in §§ 502(g), (h), or (i) Clerk shall promptly mail copy of any final order of discharge to U.S. Trustee, all creditors as provided in Rules 2002(f) and (k) and trustee and trustee's attorney.
	Vesting of all property of the estate in the debtor, free and clear of claims and interests	1141(b) 1141(c)		Except as otherwise provided in the plan or the order confirming the plan, the confirmation of a plan vests all of the property of the estate in the debtor. Except as provided in §§ 1141(d)(2) (non-dischargeable debts not discharged) and (d)(3) (cases when a liquidating debtor is not discharged) and except as otherwise provided in the plan or in the order confirming the plan, after confirmation of a plan, the property dealt with by the plan is free and clear of all claims and interests of creditors, equity security holders, and of general partners in the debtor.

DUE DATE	ACTION	CODE §	RULE	EXPLANATION; TIME TO ACT
	Effect of confirmation—termination of rights and interests of equity security holders and general partners	1141(d)(1)(B)		Except as otherwise provided in the plan or the order confirming the plan, confirmation of the plan terminates all rights and interests of equity security holders and general partners.
	Approval of written waiver of discharge in Chapter 11	1141(d)(4)		If court approves a written waiver of discharge executed by the debtor after the order for relief. Neither the Code nor the Rules specify any procedure for court approval. The debtor's plan may constitute such written agreement.
	Discharge in case in which debtor is an individual	1141(d)(5)(A)		Unless after notice and a hearing court orders otherwise for cause, confirmation of plan does not discharge any debtor until court grants discharge upon completion of payments.
	Denial of discharge in individual Chapter 11 case if § 522(q)(1) may be applicable to the debtor or proceeding pending under § 522(q)(1)(B)	1141(d)(5)(C)	Interim 2002(f)(11)	The court may not grant a discharge to an individual debtor under Chapter 11[3] unless the court, after notice and a hearing held not more than 10 days before the date of the entry of the order granting the discharge, finds that there is no reasonable cause to believe that: (1) § 522(q)(1) may be applicable to the debtor; and (2) there is pending any proceeding in which the debtor may be found guilty of a felony of the kind described in § 522(q)(1)(A) or liable for a debt of the kind described in § 522(q)(1)(B).
	Under Rule 2002(f)(11), the creditors receive notice of the time to request a delay in the entry of the discharge under § 1141(d)(5)(C). No discharge of fraud claims against corporation owed to a domestic governmental unit and tax fraud claims	1141(d)(6)		Confirmation of a plan does not discharge a debtor that is a corporation from any debt: (1) specified in paragraph of §§ 523(a)(2)(A) or (2)(B) that is owed to a domestic governmental unit; or (2) for a tax or customs duty with respect to which the debtor made a fraudulent return or willfully attempted in any manner to evade or to defeat such tax or such customs duty.
	Prerequisite to participation in distribution under plan which requires presentment or surrender of security	1143		If plan requires presentment or surrender of a security or the performance of any other act as a condition to participation in distribution under a plan, such action must be taken before 5 years after the date of entry of a confirmation order. If timely action not taken, party cannot participate in distribution under plan.

[3] The author presumes this section is meant to describe the delay in entry of the discharge, as is the case with § 1141(d)(5)(A), and as is the case with similar provisions in Chapter 13 cases, § 1328(h). However, there are words missing from § 1141(d)(5)(C), which are present in § 1328(h) which make the meaning of § 1141(d)(5)(C) unclear. Arguably, § 1141(d)(5)(C) could be read as an exception to § 1141(d)(5)(B), which grants a discharge under certain circumstances to individuals in Chapter 11 who are unable to complete payments under the plan. However, the House and Senate reports support the first meaning.

DUE DATE	ACTION	CODE §	RULE	EXPLANATION; TIME TO ACT
	Parties entitled to receive distribution under plan		3021	After confirmation of plan, to creditors whose claims have been allowed, to holders of stock, bonds, debentures, notes, and other securities of record at time of commencement of distribution whose claims or equity security interests have not been disallowed and to indenture trustees who have filed claims pursuant to Rule 3003(c)(5) that have been allowed.
	Revocation of an order of confirmation	1144	9024 7001	Court may revoke a confirmation order after notice and hearing and only if order was procured by fraud; complaint to revoke must be made before 180 days after date of entry of confirmation order.
	Time for filing complaint objecting to discharge of a debt other than under § 523(c)	523 1141(d)(2)	4007(b) 7001	Complaint may be filed at any time.
	Time for filing complaint objecting to discharge of a debt under § 523(c)	523(c) 1141(d)(2)	4007(c) 7001	Must be filed no later than 60 days following first date set for § 341(a) meeting of creditors; court must give all creditors at least 30 days notice of time so fixed in manner provided by Rule 2002; motions to extend time must be filed before expiration of period and relief granted only after notice and hearing.
	Time for filing complaint objecting to discharge; notice of time fixed		4004(a)	Complaint must be filed no later than first date set for hearing on confirmation; not less than 25 days notice of time so fixed shall be given to U.S. Trustee and all creditors as provided in Rules 2002(f) and (k), and to trustee and trustee's attorney.
	Extension of time for filing complaint objecting to discharge		4004(b)	On motion made before time has expired, and after notice and hearing, for cause.
	Notice of discharge		4004(g)	Clerk shall promptly mail copy of any final order of discharge to U.S. Trustee, all creditors as provided in Rules 2002(f) and (k) and trustee and trustee's attorney.
	Notice of no discharge		4006	After order becomes final denying or revoking the discharge or a waiver is filed, or, in the case of an individual, if the case is closed without the entry of an order of discharge, the clerk shall promptly give notice to all creditors in accordance with Rule 2002.
	Exemption from securities laws for offer or sale, other than under a plan, of a security of an issuer other than the debtor or an affiliate	1145(a)(3)		If the offer or sale is of securities that do not exceed, during the 2-year period after the petition, 4% of the securities outstanding on filing date, and during any 180-day period following the 2-year period, 1% of the securities outstanding at the beginning of the 180-day period after the filing date.

DUE DATE	ACTION	CODE §	RULE	EXPLANATION; TIME TO ACT
	Exemption from securities laws for offer or sale, other than under a plan, of a security of an issuer other than the debtor or an affiliate	1145(a)(4)		If it is a transaction by a stockbroker in a security that is executed after a transaction of a kind specified in §§ 1145(a)(1) or (2) in such security and before the expiration of 40 days after the first date on which such security was bona fide offered to the public by the issuer or by or through an underwriter, but only if the stockbroker provides, at the time or before the transaction, an approved disclosure statement with such supplements as the court orders.
	Applicability of Trust Indenture Act of 1939	1145(d)		Does not apply to notes issued under a plan that matures not later than 1 year after effective date of plan.
	Request for determination state or local tax unit of the tax effects of plan under § 346 make determination	1146(b)		Court may make determination after earlier of date the governmental unit responds or 270 days after request to governmental unit.

Chapter 13, Adjustment of Debts of an Individual with Regular Income, contains many similar topics as those in Chapter 11, only tailored to those eligible for Chapter 13 relief.

Chapter 13: Adjustment of Debts of an Individual with Regular Income

DUE DATE	ACTION	CODE §	RULE	EXPLANATION; TIME TO ACT
	Stay of action against co-debtor on a consumer debt	1301(a)		Effective after order for relief, except if such co-debtor became liable or secured the debt in the ordinary course of the debtor's business. The stay of actions against co-debtors terminates when the case is closed, dismissed or converted.
	Relief from stay against co-debtor	1301(c) 1301(d)	4001(a)	Relief granted upon motion and after notice and hearing, to the extent that the movant establishes entitlement under § 1301(c). The co-debtor stay terminates automatically 20 days after filing of motion for relief from stay under § 1301(c)(2), unless the debtor or any individual liable on the debt files and serves upon the movant a written objection.
	Chapter 13 trustee's appointment and acceptance of appointment	1302(a)	2008	If the United States trustee appoints an individual under 28 U.S.C. § 586(b) to serve as standing trustee in Chapter 13 cases and if such individual qualifies under § 322, then such individual shall serve as trustee in the case. Otherwise, the U.S. Trustee shall appoint one disinterested person to serve as trustee in the case or the U.S. Trustee may serve as a trustee. A trustee who has filed a blanket bond pursuant to Rule 2010 who does not notify court and U.S. Trustee in writing of rejection of the office within 5 days after receipt of notice of selection is deemed to have accepted the office. All others selected as trustees must notify court and U.S. Trustee in writing of acceptance of office within 5 days after receipt of notice of selection or are deemed to have rejected the office.

DUE DATE	ACTION	CODE §	RULE	EXPLANATION; TIME TO ACT
	Chapter 13 trustee's notice to the holder of a claim for a domestic support obligation and State child support enforcement agency	**1302(b)(6), (d)(1)(A), and (d)(1)(B)**		If there is a claim for a domestic support obligation, the trustee shall provide written notice to the holder: (1) of such claim; (2) of the right of such holder to use the services of the State child support enforcement agency for assistance in collecting child support during and after the case; and (3) the address and telephone number of such State child support enforcement agency. The trustee also shall provide written notice to such State child support enforcement agency: (1) of such claim; and (2) the name, address, and telephone number of such holder.
	Chapter 13 trustee's notice of discharge to holder of a claim for a domestic support obligation and State child support enforcement agency	**1302(d)(1)(C)**		If there is a claim for a domestic support obligation, trustee shall provide notice of discharge, the debtor's last known address and other information to claim holder and State child support enforcement agency, at such time when debtor is granted a discharge under § 1328.
	Filing of periodic reports	**1304(c)**	**2015(c)**	If debtor is engaged in business, debtor must file with the court, the U.S. Trustee, and any governmental unit charged with responsibility for collection or determination of any tax arising out of such operation, reports and summaries of the operation of the business, including a statement of receipts and disbursements, a statement of amounts of deductions for all taxes required to be withheld or paid for and in behalf of employees and the place where monies are deposited, and such other information as the U.S. Trustee or the court requires.
	Notice to entities known to be holding money or property subject to withdrawal or order of debtor	**1304(c)**	**2015(c)**	If debtor is engaged in business, debtor must give notice of the case to every entity known to be holding money or property subject to withdrawal or order of debtor, including every bank, savings or building and loan association, public utility company, and landlord with whom debtor has a deposit, and to every insurance company which has issued a policy having a cash surrender value payable to the debtor.
	Filing of inventory of debtor engaged in business	**1304(c)**	**2015(c)**	If the Chapter 13 debtor is engaged in business and the court directs, the debtor shall file and transmit to the U.S. Trustee.

DUE DATE	ACTION	CODE §	RULE	EXPLANATION; TIME TO ACT
	Property of Chapter 13 estate	1306		Includes all property described in § 541 plus similar property acquired and earnings from services performed by debtor post-petition but before case is closed, dismissed, or converted to Chapter 7, 11, or 12 case, whichever is first.
	Conversion to Chapter 7 by debtor	1307(a)	1017(f)(3) 9013	At any time, debtor may convert a Chapter 13 case to a Chapter 7 case. Case is automatically converted without court order on the filing by the debtor of a notice of conversion pursuant to § 1307(a), and the date of filing of the notice is deemed the date of conversion for purposes of § 348(c). The clerk shall promptly transmit the notice to the Chapter 13 trustee.
	Dismissal of case by debtor	1307(b)		At any time, if case has not been converted under §§ 706, 1112, or 1208, the debtor has an absolute right to dismissal by filing a motion served pursuant to Rule 9013.
	Conversion to Chapter 7 or dismissal of case by party in interest for cause	1307(c)	1017(f)(1)	After notice and hearing, on motion of a party in interest, the court may convert the case to Chapter 7 or dismiss the case, whichever is in the best interest, for cause. Cause includes: • unreasonable delay by the debtor prejudicial to creditors; • nonpayment of any fees and charges required under title 28, ch. 123; • failure to file a plan timely under § 1321; • failure to commence making timely payments under § 1326; • denial of confirmation of a plan under § 1325 and denial of a request made for additional time for filing another or a modified plan; • material default by the debtor with respect to a term of a confirmed plan; • revocation of the order of confirmation under § 1330, and denial of confirmation of a modified plan under § 1329; • termination of a confirmed plan by reason of the occurrence of a condition specified in the plan other than completion of payments; • failure of the debtor to pay any domestic support obligation that first becomes payable after the date of the filing of the petition.

DUE DATE	ACTION	CODE §	RULE	EXPLANATION; TIME TO ACT
	Conversion to Chapter 7 or dismissal of case by party in interest for cause—failure to timely file list of creditors, schedules and statements	1307(c)(9)	1017(c)	On request of the U.S. Trustee for failure of the debtor to file, within fifteen days, or such additional time as the court may allow, the information required by § 521[a](1)[1]
	Conversion to Chapter 7 or dismissal of case by party in interest for cause—failure to timely file statement of intention	1307(c)(10)		On request of the U.S. Trustee for failure to timely file the statement of intention under § 521(a)(2)
	Conversion to Chapter 11 or 12	1307(d)	1017(c)	Upon motion of a party in interest or U.S. Trustee, at any time before the confirmation of a plan and after notice and hearing.
	Conversion to Chapter 7 or dismissal for debtor's failure to file tax returns as required under § 1308	1307(e) 1308	1017(c)	On motion of a party in interest or the U.S. Trustee and after notice and a hearing, the court shall convert the case to Chapter 7 or dismiss the case, whichever is in best interest of creditors and estate.
	Filing of prepetition tax returns	1308(a)		Not later than day before meeting of creditors first scheduled, debtor shall file all tax returns for taxable periods ending during 4-year period ending on petition date.
	Holding open the meeting of creditors to file tax returns	1308(b)(1)		If such returns have not been filed in accordance with § 1308(a), trustee may hold open meeting to give debtor reasonable time to file the returns. Such period shall not be extended beyond: • for returns past due as of petition date, 120 days after the date of the meeting; or • for returns not past due as of petition date, the later of: (1) 120 days after the date of the meeting; or (2) date on which return is due under applicable nonbankruptcy law.
	Extension of period to file tax returns	1308(b)(2)		After notice and hearing, and ordered entered before tolling of period described in § 1308(b)(1), court may extend period to file return, if debtor demonstrates by preponderance of evidence that failure to file return was beyond control of debtor.
	Filing of plan by debtor	1321	3015(b)	May be filed with petition, but shall be filed within 15 days thereafter, and such time may not be extended except on motion of the debtor, for cause shown, on such notice as the court may direct.

[1] It is unclear the scope intended by §1307(c)(9), which still references § 521(1), which only included the list of creditors, schedules and statement of affairs. This section has been replaced by § 521(a)(1), which includes additional filing requirements on the debtor.

DUE DATE	ACTION	CODE §	RULE	EXPLANATION; TIME TO ACT
	Contents of plan- requirement of full payment of priority claims	**1322(a)(2) and (4)**		Unless the holder of a claim agrees to a different treatment, the plan must provide to pay all priority claims in full. However, a plan may provide for less than full payment of all amounts owed for a claim entitled to priority under § 507(a)(1)(B) (domestic support obligations owed to a governmental unit) only if the plan provides that all of the debtor's projected disposable income for a 5-year period beginning on the date that the first payment is due under the plan will be applied to make payments under the plan.
	Notice of hearing on confirmation		**3015(d)**	Plan or summary of plan must be included with each notice of hearing on confirmation mailed pursuant to Rule 2002(b).
	Valuation of security in cases in which the debtor is permitted to modify rights of secured creditor and/or reduce the allowed secured claim to the value of the collateral	1322(b)(2) 1322(a)(5) 506(a) and (b)	**3012**	On motion of any part in interest, after notice and hearing, the court may determine the value of the claim secured by a lien on property in which the estate has an interest. However, this does not apply to debts which are excepted from modification under §§ 1322(b)(2) (loan secured only by lien on principal residence of individual debtor) and 1325(a).
	Limit on right to cure of defaults with respect to, or that gave rise to, a lien on debtor's principal residence	**1322(c)(1)**		May be cured under §§ 1322(b)(3) or (5) until such residence is sold at a foreclosure sale that is conducted in accordance with applicable nonbankruptcy law, notwithstanding the prohibition on modification of such secured claims in § 1322(b)(2).
	Exception to rule against modification of rights of holders of claims secured only by a security interest in real property that is debtor's principal residence	**1322(c)(2)**		In a case where last payment on original payment schedule for a claim secured only by a security interest in real property that is debtor's principal residence is due before the date on which the final payment under the Chapter 13 plan is due, plan may provide for payment of the claim as modified pursuant to § 1325(a)(5), notwithstanding the prohibition on modification of such secured claims in § 1322(b)(2).

DUE DATE	ACTION	CODE §	RULE	EXPLANATION; TIME TO ACT
	Length of plan	1322(d)		If the income of the debtor and the debtor's spouse is not less than the calculation of median family income in the debtor's applicable State under the calculations of § 1322(d), the plan may not provide for payments over a period that is longer than 5 years. If the income of the debtor and the debtor's spouse is less than the calculation of median family income in the debtor's applicable State under the calculations of § 1322(d), the plan may not provide for payments over a period that is longer than 3 years, unless the court, for cause, approves a longer period, not to exceed 5 years. *See* § 1325 (b) (requiring dedication of the all disposable income for the applicable commitment period unless all claims are paid in full by an earlier time).
	Modification of plan before confirmation	1323(a)		Debtor may modify plan at any time before confirmation.
	Determination of classes of creditors and equity security holders	1322(b)(1)	3013	The plan may provide for classification of claims or interests or on motion of a party in interest, after notice and a hearing, the court may determine the classification of claims and interests.
	Objections to confirmation of plan	1324	3015(f) 9014	Must be filed and served on debtor, trustee, and any other entity designated by court, and transmitted to U.S. Trustee before confirmation.
	Confirmation without objection	1325		Court must find each of the applicable requirements of § 1325 has been met, but if there is no objection to confirmation is timely filed, the court may determine that the plan was proposed in good faith and not by any means forbidden by law without receiving evidence on these issues.
	Notice of confirmation hearing	1324(a)	3015(d)	After notice as provided in Rule 2002(b).
	Timing of confirmation hearing	1324(b)		Between 20 and 45 days from meeting of creditors, unless court determines that it would be in best interest of creditors and estate to hold hearing earlier and there is no objection to earlier date.

DUE DATE	ACTION	CODE §	RULE	EXPLANATION; TIME TO ACT
	Requirement of confirmation—payment of certain purchase money secured debts without the benefit of valuation of secured claim under § 506	1325(a)(5)		For purposes of § 1325(a)(5), § 506 shall not apply if the creditor has a purchase money security interest securing the debt, the debt was incurred within the 910-day period preceding the date of the filing of the petition, and the collateral consists of a motor vehicle acquired for the personal use of the debtor, or if collateral consists of any other thing of value, if the debt was incurred during the 1-year period preceding that filing.
	Requirement of confirmation—payment of postpetition domestic support obligations	1325(a)(8)		The court shall confirm the plan only if the debtor has paid all amounts that are required to be paid under a domestic support obligation and that first become payable after the date of the filing of the petition if the debtor is required by a judicial or administrative order, or by statute, to pay such domestic support obligation.
	Requirement for confirmation of the plan—filing all tax returns required by § 1308	1325(a)(9)		The court shall confirm the plan only if the debtor has filed all applicable federal, state, and local tax returns as required by § 1308.
	Confirmation of plan over objection of the trustee or unsecured creditor—requirement for dedication of all disposable income	1325(b)(1)		If the trustee or the holder of an allowed unsecured claim objects to the confirmation of the plan, then the court may not approve the plan unless, as of the effective date of the plan: (1) the value of the property to be distributed under the plan on account of such claim is not less than the amount of such claim; or (2) the plan provides that all of the debtor's projected disposable income to be received in the applicable commitment period beginning on the date that the first payment is due under the plan will be applied to make payments to unsecured creditors under the plan.
	Calculation of applicable commitment period	1325(b)(4)		If the income of the debtor and the debtor's spouse is not less than the calculation of median family income in the debtor's applicable State under the calculations of § 1325(b)(4)(A), the applicable commitment period shall be not less than 5 years. In all other cases, the applicable commitment period shall be 3 years. However, the applicable commitment period may be shorter than 3 or 5 years if the plan provides for full payment of unsecured claims over a shorter period.
	Commencement of payments by debtor to trustee	1326(a)(1)		Debtor must commence making payments not later than 30 days after date the plan is filed or order of relief, whichever is earlier.

DUE DATE	ACTION	CODE §	RULE	EXPLANATION; TIME TO ACT
	Distributions of payments by trustee	1326(a)(2)		After a plan is confirmed, the trustee distributes payments in accordance with plan, as soon as is practicable. If a plan is not confirmed, the trustee shall return any such payments not previously paid and not yet due and owing to creditors pursuant to § 1326(a)(3) to the debtor, after deducting any unpaid claim allowed under § 503(b).
	Modification of payments pending confirmation	1326(a)(3)		Subject to § 363, the court may, upon notice and a hearing, modify, increase, or reduce the payments required under 1326(a)(1)(A) pending confirmation of a plan.
	Duty of debtor to provide proof of insurance coverage on personal property to lessor of or holder of purchase money security interest in personal property in debtor's possession	1326(a)(4)		Not later than 60 days after filing of case under Chapter 13, a debtor retaining possession of personal property subject to a lease or securing a claim attributable in whole or in part to the purchase price of such property shall provide the lessor or secured creditor reasonable evidence of the maintenance of any required insurance coverage with respect to the use or ownership of such property and continue to do so for so long as the debtor retains possession of such property.
	Effect of confirmation on property	1327(b) 1327(c)		Except as otherwise provided in the plan or confirmation order, the confirmation of the plan automatically vests all property of the estate in the debtor free and clear of any claim or interest.
	Granting of discharge (except as to debts listed in § 1328(a))	1328(a)		Subject to the exceptions in § 1328(d), as soon as practicable after completion by the debtor of all payments under the plan, and in case of debtor required to pay domestic support obligations, after debtor certifies that all domestic support obligations due on or before date of certification, including the amounts due before the petition was filed to the extent provided by the plan, have been paid.
	Hardship discharge	1328(b)		Subject to the exceptions in § 1328(d), upon motion any time after confirmation of the plan and after notice and a hearing, court may grant a discharge to a debtor that has not completed payments under the plan, subject to the conditions in 1328(b).
	Time for filing complaint for determination of dischargeability of a debt other than under § 523(c)	1328(a)	4007(b)	A debtor or any creditor may file a complaint at any time to determine whether a debt not covered under § 523(c) is dischargeable. A case may be reopened without payment of an additional filing fee to obtain such determination.

DUE DATE	ACTION	CODE §	RULE	EXPLANATION; TIME TO ACT
	Time for filing complaint for determination of dischargeability of a debt under § 523(c) and not discharged under § 1328(a)	**1328(a)** **523(a)(2)** **523(a)(4)**	**Interim 4007(c)**	Except as provided in Rule 4007(d), a complaint to determine the dischargeability of a debt under § 523(c) shall be filed no later than 60 days after the first date set for the meeting of creditors under § 341(a). The court shall give all creditors no less than 30 days' notice of the time so fixed in the manner provided in Rule 2002. On motion of any party in interest, after hearing on notice, the court may for cause extend the time. The motion shall be filed before the time has expired.
	Time for filing complaint for determination of dischargeability of a debt under § 523(a)(6) when debtor is seeking a hardship discharge	**1328(b)** **523(a)(6)** **523(c)**	**Interim 4007(d)** **7001**	On motion by a debtor for a discharge under § 1328(b), the court shall enter an order fixing the time to file a complaint to determine the dischargeability of any debt under § 523(a)(6) and shall give no less than 30 days' notice of the time fixed to all creditors in the manner provided in Rule 2002. On motion of any party in interest after hearing on notice the court may for cause extend the time. The motion shall be filed before the time has expired.
	Revocation of discharge	**1328(e)**	**7001**	Court may revoke the discharge on request of party in interest before 1 year after a discharge is granted, and after notice and hearing, if discharge obtained through fraud.
	Denial of discharge if prior discharge during applicable periods	**1328(f)**		The court shall not grant a discharge of all debts provided for in the plan or disallowed under § 502, if the debtor has received a discharge: (1) in a case filed under Chapter 7, 11, or 12 during the 4-year period preceding the date of the order for relief; or (2) in a case filed under Chapter 13 during the 2-year period preceding the date of the order for relief.
	Denial of discharge for failure to complete instructional course in personal financial management	**1328(g)**	**Interim 1006(b)(7) and (c)**	Discharge denied if debtor fails to complete instructional course described in § 111, unless the debtor is a person described in § 109(h)(4) or who resides in a district where approval instructional courses are not adequate. Unless the U.S. Trustee has determined that the requirement does not apply in the district, the debtor shall file a statement regarding completion of a course in personal financial management, prepared as prescribed by the appropriate Official Form no later than the last payment made by the debtor as required by the plan or the filing of a motion for entry of a discharge under § 1328(b).

DUE DATE	ACTION	CODE §	RULE	EXPLANATION; TIME TO ACT
	Denial of discharge in Chapter 13 case if § 522(q)(1) may be applicable to the debtor or proceeding pending under § 522(q)(1)(B)	1328(h)	Interim 2002(f)(11)	The court may not grant a discharge unless the court, after notice and a hearing held not more than 10 days before the date of the entry of the order granting the discharge, finds that there is no reasonable cause to believe that: (1) § 522(q)(1) may be applicable to the debtor; and (2) there is pending any proceeding in which the debtor may be found guilty of a felony of the kind described in § 522(q)(1)(A) or liable for a debt of the kind described in § 522(q)(1)(B). Under Rule 2002(f)(11), the creditors receive notice of the time to request a delay in the entry of the discharge under §§ 1141(d)(5)(C).
	Delay of order of discharge if debtor has not filed statement concerning § 522(q)		Interim 4004(c)(3)[2]	If the debtor is required to file a statement under Interim Rule 1007(b)(8), the court shall not grant a discharge earlier than 30 days after the filing of the statement.
	Notice of order denying or revoking discharge, or of waiver of discharge		4006	After order becomes final or waiver is filed, clerk shall promptly give notice to all creditors in accordance with Rule 2002.
	Modification of plan after confirmation	1329(a)		After notice and hearing, at any time after confirmation of the plan but before the completion of payments under the plan.
	Limitation on duration of modified plan	1329(c)		Plan as modified may not have payments over a period that expires after the applicable commitment period under § 1325(b)(1)(B) after the time that the first payment under the original confirmed plan was due, unless court, for cause, approves longer time, but court may not approve a period that expires after 5 years after such time.
	Revocation of an order of confirmation procured by fraud	1330	7001	On request of party in interest at any time within 180 days after date of entry of confirmation order under § 1325 and after notice and hearing; if court revokes confirmation order, court shall convert or dismiss case unless debtor timely proposes and the court confirms a modification of the plan.

[2] This modification to the Interim Rules was proposed on October 13, 2005. Check your court's local rule to determine whether this Interim Rule was adopted as part of its local rules.

Chapter 15, Ancillary And Other Cross-Border Cases, is a new chapter that contains those provisions applicable to cross border cases and issues, including ancillary cases, foreign representatives, notification of foreign creditors, recognition of foreign proceedings and relief, and concurrent proceedings.

Chapter 15: Ancillary and Other Cross-Border Cases

DUE DATE	ACTION	CODE §	RULE	EXPLANATION; TIME TO ACT
	Foreign main proceeding	**1502(4)**		A foreign proceeding pending in the country where the debtor has the center of its main interests.
	Foreign nonmain proceeding	**1502(5)**		A foreign proceeding, other than a foreign main proceeding, pending in a country where the debtor has an establishment.
	Commencement of an ancillary case	**1504 1515(a)**		A case under this chapter is commenced by the filing of a petition for recognition of a foreign proceeding by the foreign representative under § 1515.
	Appointment of a foreign representative	**1515(a)**		A foreign representative is appointed in the foreign proceeding for which recognition is sought.
	Documents accompanying petition for recognition	**1515(b) and (c)**		A petition for recognition shall be accompanied by: (1) (a) a certified copy of the decision commencing such foreign proceeding and appointing the foreign representative; (b) a certificate from the foreign court affirming the existence of such foreign proceeding and of the appointment of the foreign representative; or (c) in the absence of this type of evidence, any other evidence acceptable to the court of the existence of such foreign proceeding and of the appointment of the foreign representative; and (2) a statement identifying all foreign proceedings with respect to the debtor that are known to the foreign representative.
	List of creditors filed with petition		**Interim 1007(a)(4)**	Unless the court orders otherwise, a foreign representative filing a petition for recognition under Chapter 15 shall file with the petition a list containing the name and address of all administrators in foreign proceedings of the debtor, all parties to any litigation in which the debtor is a party and that is pending in the U.S. at the time of the filing of the petition, and all entities against whom provisional relief is being sought under § 1519.

DUE DATE	ACTION	CODE §	RULE	EXPLANATION; TIME TO ACT
	Procedure upon filing a petition for recognition of a foreign nonmain proceeding[1]		**Interim 1010**	On the filing of a petition for recognition of a foreign nonmain proceeding the clerk shall forthwith issue a summons for service. When a petition for recognition of a foreign nonmain proceeding is filed, service shall be made on the debtor, any entity against whom provisional relief is sought under § 1519, and on any other parties as the court may direct. The summons shall be served with a copy of the petition in the manner provided for service of a summons and complaint by Rule 7004(a).
	Notice of petition for recognition of foreign proceeding		**Interim 2002(q)(1)**	The clerk, or some other person as the court may direct, shall forthwith give the debtor, all administrators in foreign proceedings of the debtor, all entities against whom provisional relief is being sought under § 1519, all parties to any litigation in which the debtor is a party and that is pending in the U.S. at the time of the filing of the petition, and such other entities as the court may direct, at least 20 days notice by mail of the hearing on the petition for recognition of a foreign proceeding. The notice shall state whether the petition seeks recognition as a foreign main proceeding or foreign nonmain proceeding.
	Contest of a petition for recognition			A party in interest to a petition for foreign recognition may contest the petition by filing an answer or motion under Rule 1012(b) and FRP 12 within 20 days after service of the summons.[2]
	Foreign representatives right to commence bankruptcy case	1511		Upon recognition, a foreign representative may commence: (1) an involuntary case under § 303; or (2) a voluntary case under §§ 301 or 302, if the foreign proceeding is a foreign main proceeding. The petition commencing a case must be accompanied by a certified copy of an order granting recognition. The court where the petition for recognition has been filed must be advised of the foreign representative's intent to commence a case prior to such commencement.

[1] Interim Rule 1010 specifies the issuance of a summons and service only for foreign nonmain proceedings, although Interim Rule 1011 provides for the debtor's right to contest any petition for recognition within 20 days after service of the summons. It is not clear whether Rule 1010 or any other rule expressly provides for issuance of a summons for a foreign main proceeding.

[2] Interim Rule 1010 specifies the issuance of a summons and service only for foreign nonmain proceedings, although Interim Rule 1011 provides for the debtor's right to contest any petition for recognition within 20 days after service of the summons. It is not clear whether Rule 1010 or any other rule expressly provides for issuance of a summons for a foreign main proceeding.

DUE DATE	ACTION	CODE §	RULE	EXPLANATION; TIME TO ACT
	Participation of foreign representative in a bankruptcy case	1512		Upon recognition of a foreign proceeding, the foreign representative is entitled as a party in interest in any bankruptcy case under Title 11 regarding the debtor.
	Notice to foreign creditors of bankruptcy case	1514		Notification to creditors with foreign addresses shall be given individually, unless the court considers that, under the circumstances, some other form of notification would be more appropriate. No letter or other formality is required. When a notification of commencement of a case is to be given to foreign creditors, such notification shall: (1) indicate the time period for filing proofs of claim and specify the place for filing such proofs of claim; (2) indicate whether secured creditors need to file proofs of claim; and (3) contain any other information required to be included in such notification to creditors under the Code and the orders of the court.
	Enlargement of time prescribed by notice to accommodate foreign creditors	1514(d)	Interim 2002(p)	If, at the request of a party in interest or the U.S. Trustee, or on its own initiative, the court finds that a notice mailed within the time prescribed by these rules would not be sufficient to give a creditor with a foreign address to which notices under these rules are mailed reasonable notice under the circumstances, the court may order that the notice be supplemented with notice by other means or that the time prescribed for the notice by mail be enlarged. Unless the court for cause orders otherwise, a creditor with a foreign address to which notices under this rule are mailed shall be given at least 30 days notice of the time fixed for filing a proof of claim under Rules 3002(c) or 3003(c).
	Entry of an order recognizing a foreign proceeding	1517(a) 1506 1515		Subject to § 1506 (refusal to grant recognition if relief manifestly contrary to public policy), after notice and a hearing, the court shall grant recognition if: (1) such foreign proceeding for which recognition is sought is a foreign main proceeding or foreign nonmain proceeding; (2) the foreign representative applying for recognition is a person or body; and (3) the petition meets the requirements of § 1515.
	Time for deciding petition for recognition of foreign proceeding	1517(c)		A petition for recognition of foreign proceeding shall be decided at the earliest possible time.

DUE DATE	ACTION	CODE §	RULE	EXPLANATION; TIME TO ACT
	Modification or termination of order of recognition.	1517(d)		The court may modify or terminate recognition if it is shown that the grounds for granting it were fully or partially lacking or have ceased to exist, but in considering such action the court shall give due weight to possible prejudice to parties that have relied upon the order granting recognition.
	Closing of a Chapter 15 case	1517(d)		A case under this chapter may be closed in the manner prescribed under § 350.
	Notice of change of status	1518	2015(d)	The foreign representative shall file with the court a notice of change of status concerning any substantial change in the status of such foreign proceeding or the status of the foreign representative's appointment; and any other foreign proceeding regarding the debtor within 15 days after the date when the representative becomes aware of the subsequent information.
	Provisional relief that may be granted upon filing of petition for recognition	1519(a)		Subject to §§ 1519(c), (d) and (f), from the time of filing of the petition until the court rules on the petition, the court may, at the request of the foreign representative, where relief is urgently needed to protect the assets of the debtor or the interests of the creditors, grant relief of a provisional nature specified in § 1519(a). The standards, procedures, and limitations applicable to an injunction shall apply to relief under § 1519.
	Termination of provisional relief	1519(b)		Unless extended under § 1521(a)(6) as relief granted upon recognition, the relief granted under § 1519 terminates when the petition for recognition is granted.

DUE DATE	ACTION	CODE §	RULE	EXPLANATION; TIME TO ACT
	Effect of recognition of a foreign main proceeding	**1520**		Upon recognition of a foreign proceeding that is a foreign main proceeding: • §§ 361 and 362 apply with respect to the debtor and the property of the debtor that is within the territorial jurisdiction of the U.S.; • §§ 363, 549, and 552 apply to a transfer of an interest of the debtor in property that is within the territorial jurisdiction of the U.S. to the same extent that the sections would apply to property of an estate; • unless the court orders otherwise, the foreign representative may operate the debtor's business and may exercise the rights and powers of a trustee under and to the extent provided by §§ 363 and 552; and • § 552 applies to property of the debtor that is within the territorial jurisdiction of the U.S.
	Additional discretionary relief upon recognition	**1521(a)** **1523**		Upon recognition of foreign proceeding and at request or foreign representative, where necessary to effectuate the purpose of Chapter 15 and to protect the assets of the debtor or the interests of the creditors, the court may, at the request of the foreign representative, grant any appropriate relief as described in § 1521(a), including relief available to trustee, other than the avoidance powers. However, if a bankruptcy case is pending under another chapter, the foreign representative has standing to initiate actions under §§ 522, 544, 545, 547, 548, 550, 553, and 724(a), subject to § 1523(b).
	Entrustment of distribution of domestic assets to foreign representative or other person	**1521(b)**		Upon recognition of a foreign proceeding, the court may, on motion of the foreign representative, entrust the distribution of all or part of the debtor's assets located in the U.S. to the foreign representative or another person, including an examiner, provided that the court is satisfied that the interests of creditors in the U.S. are sufficiently protected.
	Modification or termination of relief under §§ 1519 or 1521	**1522**		On the motion of the foreign representative or any entity affected by the relief under §§ 1519 or 1521, or on its own motion, the court may modify or terminate such relief.
	Authority of foreign representative to intervene	**1524**		Upon recognition of a foreign proceeding, the foreign representative may intervene in any proceedings in a state or federal court in the U.S. in which the debtor is a party.

DUE DATE	ACTION	CODE §	RULE	EXPLANATION; TIME TO ACT
	Direct communication between the court and foreign court or foreign representative	1525		The court shall cooperate to the maximum extent possible with a foreign court or a foreign representative, either directly or through the trustee. The court is entitled to communicate directly with, or to request information or assistance directly from, a foreign court or a foreign representative, subject to the rights of a party in interest to notice and participation.
	Notice of court's intention to communicate with foreign courts and foreign representatives		**Interim 2002(q)(2)**	The clerk, or some other person as the court may direct, shall give the debtor, all administrators in foreign proceedings of the debtor, all entities against whom provisional relief is being sought under § 1519, all parties to any litigation in which the debtor is a party and that is pending in the U.S. at the time of the filing of the petition, and such other entities as the court may direct, notice by mail of the court's intention to communicate with a foreign court or foreign representative as prescribed by Rule 5012.
	Procedure for participation in communication with foreign court or foreign representative		**Interim 5012**	Except for communications for scheduling and administrative purposes, the court in any case commenced by a foreign representative shall give at least 20 days notice of its intent to communicate with a foreign court or a foreign representative. The notice shall identify the subject of the anticipated communication and shall be given in the manner provided by Rule 2002(q). Any entity that wishes to participate in the communication shall notify the court of its intention not later than 5 days before the scheduled communication.
	Limitation on commencement of a bankruptcy case after recognition of a foreign main proceeding	1528		After recognition of a foreign main proceeding, a case under another chapter may be commenced only if the debtor has assets in the U.S.
	Restriction on effects of bankruptcy case commenced after recognition of a foreign main proceeding	1528		The effects of case commenced after recognition of a foreign main proceeding shall be restricted to the assets of the debtor that are within the territorial jurisdiction of the U.S. and, to the extent necessary to implement cooperation and coordination, to other assets of the debtor that are within the jurisdiction of the court under § 541(a) and 28 USC § 1334(e), to the extent that such other assets are not subject to the jurisdiction and control of a foreign proceeding that has been recognized under Chapter 15.

The material in this chapter describes deadlines contained in the rules applicable to appeals, including to District courts and Bankruptcy Appellate Panels, including deadlines to file appeals and briefing.

Rules for Appeals

DUE DATE	ACTION	CODE §	RULE	EXPLANATION; TIME TO ACT
	Appeals heard by district court	**28 USC 158(a)**		
	Appeals heard by Bankruptcy Appellate Panel (BAP) (where applicable)	**28 USC § 158(c)(1)**	**8001(e)**	Subject to 28 USC § 158(b), each appeal under 28 USC § 158(a) shall be heard by a 3-judge panel of the bankruptcy appellate panel service, unless: (a) the appellant elects at the time of the filing of the appeal; or (b) any other party elects, not later than 30 days after service of the notice of appeal, to have such appeal heard by the district court.
	Direct appeals to the Court of Appeals from judgments, orders and decrees of the bankruptcy court	**28 USC 158(d)**		The appropriate court of appeals shall have jurisdiction of appeals described in the first sentence of § 158(a) if the bankruptcy court, the district court, or the bankruptcy appellate panel involved, acting on its own motion or on the request of a party to the judgment, order, or decree described in such first sentence, or all the appellants and appellees (if any) acting jointly, certify that: (1) the judgment, order, or decree involves a question of law as to which there is no controlling decision of the court of appeals for the circuit or of the Supreme Court, or involves a matter of public importance; (2) the judgment, order, or decree involves a question of law requiring resolution of conflicting decisions; or (3) an immediate appeal from the judgment, order, or decree may materially advance the progress of the case or proceeding in which the appeal is taken; and if the court of appeals authorizes the direct appeal of the judgment, order, or decree.

DUE DATE	ACTION	CODE §	RULE	EXPLANATION; TIME TO ACT
	Certification for direct appeal to Court of Appeals	**28 USC § 158(d)(2)**	**Interim 8001(f)(1) and (2)**	A certification of a judgment, order, or decree of a bankruptcy court to a court of appeals under 28 USC § 158(d)(2) is ineffective until a timely appeal has been taken in the manner required by Rules 8001(a) and (b). A certification that a circumstance specified in 28 USC §§ 158(d)(2)(A)(i)–(iii) exists shall be made in the court in which a matter is pending for purposes of 28 USC § 158(d)(2). A matter is pending in a bankruptcy court until the docketing, in accordance with Rule 8007(b), of an appeal taken under 28 USC § 158(a)(1) or (2), or the grant of leave to appeal under 28 USC § 158(a)(3). A matter is pending in a district court or bankruptcy appellate panel after the docketing, in accordance with Rule 8007(b), of an appeal taken under 28 USC § 158(a)(1) or (2), or the grant of leave to appeal under 28 USC § 158(a)(3). Only a bankruptcy court may make a certification on request or on its own initiative until the earlier of the docketing of the appeal in accordance with Rule 8007(b) or the grant of leave to appeal under 28 USC § 158(a). After an appeal has been docketed in accordance with Rule 8007(b) or leave to appeal has been granted under 28 USC § 158(a), only the district court or bankruptcy appellate panel involved may make a certification on request of the parties or on its own initiative. A certification by all the appellants and appellees, if any, acting jointly may be made by filing the appropriate Official Form with the clerk of the court in which the matter is pending. The certification may be accompanied by a short statement of the basis for the certification, which may include the information listed in Interim Rule 8001(f)(3)(C).

DUE DATE	ACTION	CODE §	RULE	EXPLANATION; TIME TO ACT
	Request for certification of direct appeal	**28 USC § 158(d)(2)(E)**	**Interim 8001(f)(3)**	A request for certification shall be filed, within 60 days of entry of the order, judgment or decree, with the clerk of the court in which the matter is pending. Notice of the filing of a request for certification shall be served in the manner required for service of a notice of appeal under Rule 8004. A party may file a response to a request for certification or a cross-request within 10 days after the notice of the request is served, or another time fixed by the court.
	Form of request for certification	**28 USC § 158(d)(2)(A)**	**Interim 8001(f)(4)**	A certification of an appeal on the court's own initiative under 28 USC § 158(d)(2) shall be made in a separate document served on the parties in the manner required for service of a notice of appeal under Rule 8004. The certification shall be accompanied by an opinion or memorandum that contains the information required by subdivision (f)(3)(C)(i)–(iv) of Rule 8001. A party may file a supplementary short statement of the basis for certification within 10 days after the certification.
	Time for filing notice of appeal		**8002(a)**	Must be filed with clerk within 10 days of date of entry of judgment, order, or decree appealed from; if a timely notice of appeal is filed, any other party may file a notice of appeal within 10 days of the date on which the first notice of appeal was filed, or within time otherwise prescribed in Rule 8002, whichever last expires; notice of appeal filed after the announcement of a decision or order but before entry of the judgment, order, or decree is treated as filed after such entry and on the date of entry.
	Time for filing notice of appeal when after motion to amend		**8002(b)**	If timely motion is filed by any party under Rules 7052(b) (amend or make additional findings of fact), 9023 (alter or amend judgment), or 9023 (for new trial), the time for appeal for all parties shall run from entry of order disposing of last such motion outstanding.

DUE DATE	ACTION	CODE §	RULE	EXPLANATION; TIME TO ACT
	Extension of time		**8002(c)**	Bankruptcy judge may extend time for filing notice of appeal by any party for period not to exceed 20 days from expiration of time otherwise prescribed by Rule 8002 (or 10 days from entry of order granting the extension request, whichever is later); request to extend time must be made before time for filing notice of appeal has expired, except that a request made no more than 20 days after the expiration of the time for filing a notice of appeal may be granted upon a showing of excusable neglect, unless the judgment or order appealed from: (A) grants relief from the automatic stay; (B) authorizes the sale of property or the use of cash collateral; (C) authorizes the obtaining of credit under § 364; (D) authorizes the assumption or assignment of any executory contract or unexpired lease under § 365; (E) approves a disclosure statement under § 1125; or (F) confirms a plan under §§ 943, 1129, or 1325.
	Motion for leave to appeal; answer; transmittal		**8003(a)**	Answer in opposition to motion for leave to appeal under 28 USC § 158(a) must be filed within 10 days after service of the motion.
			8003(b)	Clerk must transmit notice of appeal, motion for leave to appeal, and answer to clerk of district court or BAP as soon as all parties have filed answers or time for filing answers has expired. Motion and answer shall be submitted without oral argument unless otherwise ordered.
			8003(c)	If motion for leave to appeal is not filed, but notice of appeal is, notice is treated as motion, unless court orders motion to be filed; if court orders motion to be filed, it must be done within 10 days of entry of order.
			Interim 8003(d)	If leave to appeal is required by 28 USC § 158(a) and has not earlier been granted, the authorization of a direct appeal by a court of appeals under 28 USC § 158(d)(2) shall be deemed to satisfy the requirement for leave to appeal.
	Election to have appeal heard by District Court instead of Bankruptcy Appellate Panel		**8001(e)**	May be given in separate statement of consent executed by a party or contained in notice of appeal or cross appeal.

DUE DATE	ACTION	CODE §	RULE	EXPLANATION; TIME TO ACT
	Voluntary dismissal of appeal		8001(c)	If appeal has not been docketed, appeal may be dismissed by bankruptcy judge on filing of stipulation for dismissal signed by all parties, or on motion made and notice by appellant. If appeal has been docketed and parties to appeal sign and file with clerk of district court or BAP an agreement to dismiss appeal and pay court costs or fees due, clerk of district court or BAP must enter order dismissing appeal; if no agreement, appeal may be dismissed on motion of appellant on terms and conditions fixed by district court or BAP.
	Stay Pending Appeal		8005	A motion for a stay of the judgment, order, or decree of a bankruptcy judge, for approval of a supersedeas bond, or for other relief pending appeal must ordinarily be presented to the bankruptcy judge in the first instance (and not the district court or bankruptcy appellate panel).
	Designation of record and issues on appeal		8006	Within 10 days after filing of notice of appeal, entry of order granting leave to appeal, or entry of order disposing of last timely Rule 8002(b) motion, whichever is later, appellant must file with the clerk and serve on appellee a designation of items to be included in the record on appeal and a statement of issues to be presented. Within 10 days after service of appellant's designation, appellee may file and serve on appellant designation of additional items to be included in record and, if appellee has filed a cross appeal, the appellee/cross appellant shall file and serve a statement of issues to be presented on cross appeal and a designation of additional items to be included in record. Cross appellee may, within 10 days of service of statement of cross appellant, file and serve on cross appellant a designation of additional items to be included in record. If record designated by any party includes a transcript, party shall immediately after filing the designation deliver to the reporter and file with the clerk a written request for the transcript and make arrangements for payment.

DUE DATE	ACTION	CODE §	RULE	EXPLANATION; TIME TO ACT
	Duty of reporter to prepare and file transcript		8007(a)	On receipt of request for transcript, reporter must acknowledge on the request the date received and date on which reporter expects to have transcript completed; endorsed request shall be transmitted to clerk or BAP. On completion of transcript, reporter must file with clerk; if transcript cannot be completed within 30 days of receipt of request, reporter must seek extension of time from clerk and the action of the clerk must be entered on the docket and the parties notified; clerk must notify judge if reporter does not timely deliver.
	Duty of clerk to transmit copy of record; docketing of appeal		8007(b)	When record is complete, bankruptcy clerk transmits a copy to clerk of district court or BAP. On receipt of record, district court or BAP clerk must enter the appeal in the docket and give notice promptly to all parties to the judgment, order, or decree appealed from of the date on which the appeal was docketed.
	Filing and Service		8008	Papers required or permitted to be filed with the clerk of the district court or the clerk of the bankruptcy appellate panel may be filed by mail addressed to the clerk, but filing is not timely unless the papers are received by the clerk within the time fixed for filing, except that briefs are deemed to filed on the day of mailing.
	Briefs		8009	Appellant must serve and file opening brief within 15 days after entry of appeal on docket in accordance with Rule 8007; appellant must serve and file required appendix with opening brief (only if appeal is to BAP). Appellee must serve and file answering brief within 15 days after service of opening brief; if appellee has filed a cross appeal, brief of appellee must also contain issues and argument pertinent to cross appeal. Appellant may serve and file reply brief within 10 days after service of answering brief, and if appellee has cross-appealed, appellee may file and serve a reply brief to the response of the appellant to the issues presented in the cross appeal within 10 days after service of the reply brief.

DUE DATE	ACTION	CODE §	RULE	EXPLANATION; TIME TO ACT
	Motions; response		8011(a)	A request for an order or other relief must be made by filing with clerk a motion with proof of service on all other parties to appeal; if motion is supported by briefs, affidavits or other papers, they must be served and filed with the motion. Any party may file a response to a motion other than one for a procedural order within 7 days after service of the motion.
	Determination of motions for procedural orders		8011(b)	Motions for procedural orders, including any motion under Rule 9006, may be acted on at any time, without awaiting a response and without hearing.
	Motion for rehearing		8015	May be filed within 10 days after entry of the judgment; if timely motion for rehearing is filed, the 10-day period to appeal will not end for any party (not just the movant) until 10 days after the entry of an order denying rehearing or entry of subsequent judgment.
	Entry of judgment		8016(a)	Clerk of district court or BAP shall prepare, sign, and enter judgment following receipt of opinion of the court or, if there is no opinion, following the instruction of the court; notation of judgment in the docket constitutes entry of judgment.
	Notice of orders or judgments		8016(b)	Immediately on entry of judgment or order, clerk shall transmit notice of entry to each party on the appeal, the U.S. Trustee, and to the clerk, together with a copy of any opinion respecting the judgment or order.
	Automatic stay of judgment on appeal		8017(a)	Judgments of the district court or BAP are stayed until expiration of 10 days after entry.
	Stay pending appeal to Court of Appeals		8017(b)	After notice and motion, district court or BAP may stay judgment pending an appeal; stay shall not extend beyond 30 days after entry of judgment unless period is extended for cause, except that if before expiration of stay an appeal to court of appeals is filed by party obtaining stay, stay shall continue until final disposition by court of appeals (bond may be required).

This section contains deadlines associated with miscellaneous other rules applicable in bankruptcy cases, including notice to creditors and other parties in interest for all types of motions and actions, computation of time, service of pleadings, and removal proceedings.

Miscellaneous Rules

DUE DATE	ACTION	CODE §	RULE	EXPLANATION; TIME TO ACT
	Actions requiring at least 20 days notice by mail to debtor, trustee, all creditors, and indenture trustees		2002(a)	• § 341(a) meeting of creditors; • Proposed use, sale, or lease of property of the estate other than in the ordinary course of business; • Hearing on approval of compromise or settlement of controversy other than approval of agreement pursuant to Rule 4001(d); • Date fixed for filing claims against a surplus in estate as provided for in Rule 3002(c)(6); • In Chapter 7 or 11, hearing on dismissal of case (unless dismissal pursuant to § 707(b)) or conversion to another chapter; • Time fixed to accept or reject proposed modification of plan; • Hearings on all applications for compensation or reimbursement of expenses totaling in excess of $500; and • Time fixed for filing proofs of claim pursuant to Rule 3003(c).
	Actions requiring at least 25 days notice by mail to debtor, trustee, all creditors, and indenture trustees		2002(b)	• Time fixed for filing objections and the hearing to consider approval of a disclosure statement • Time fixed for filing objections and hearing to consider confirmation of Chapter 11 or 13 plan.
	Actions requiring notice to equity security holders in Chapter 11 cases by clerk or other person directed by court		2002(d)	• Order for relief; • Any § 341 meeting of equity holders; • Hearing on proposed sale of all or substantially all of debtor's assets; • Hearing on dismissal or conversion of case to another chapter; • Time fixed for filing objections to and hearing to consider approval of disclosure statement; • Time fixed for filing objections to and hearing to consider confirmation of plan; • Time fixed to accept or reject proposed modification of plan.

DUE DATE	ACTION	CODE §	RULE	EXPLANATION; TIME TO ACT
	Other notices required to be given by mail to debtor, all creditors, and indenture trustees by the clerk or other person directed by court		2002(f)	• Order for relief; • Dismissal or conversion of case to another chapter or the suspension of proceedings under § 305; • Time allowed for filing claims pursuant to Rule 3002; • Time fixed for filing complaint objecting to debtor's discharge pursuant to § 727 as provided in Rule 4004; • Time fixed for filing complaint to determine dischargeability of a debt pursuant to § 523 as provided in Rule 4007; • Waiver, denial, or revocation of discharge as provided in Rule 4006; • Entry of order confirming Chapter 11 plan as provided in Rule 3020(c); • Summary of trustee's final report and account in Chapter 7 case if net proceeds realized exceed $1,500; • The time to request a delay in the entry of the discharge under §§ 1141(d)(5)(C) and 1328(h).
	Actions requiring notice to official committees		2002(i)	Copies of all 2002 notices should be mailed to §§ 705 and 1102 committees; A committee appointed under § 1114 shall receive copies of all notices required by Rules 2002(a)(1), (a)(5), (b), (f)(2), and (f)(7), and such other notices as the court may direct.
	Action requiring notices to the United States		2002(j)	Copies of notices required to be mailed to all creditors under Rule 2002 shall be mailed: • in a Chapter 11 reorganization case, to the Securities and Exchange Commission; • in a commodity broker case, to the Commodity Futures Trading Commission at Washington, D.C.; • in a Chapter 11 case, to the Internal Revenue Service at its address set out in the register maintained under Rule 5003(e) for the district in which the case is pending; • if the papers in the case disclose a debt to the United States other than for taxes, to the U.S. attorney for the district in which the case is pending and to the department, agency, or instrumentality of the United States through which the debtor became indebted; • if the filed papers disclose a stock interest of the United States, to the Secretary of the Treasury at Washington, D.C.

DUE DATE	ACTION	CODE §	RULE	EXPLANATION; TIME TO ACT
	Actions requiring notice to U.S. Trustee		**2002(k)**	Unless the case is a Chapter 9 municipality case or unless the U.S. Trustee requests otherwise, the clerk, or some other person as the court may direct, shall transmit to the U.S. Trustee notice of the matters described in Rules 2002(a)(2), (a)(3), (a)(4), (a)(8), (b), (f)(1), (f)(2), (f)(4), (f)(6), (f)(7), and (f)(8) within the Rule 2002(a) and (b) time limits.
	Notice of order for relief in voluntary case commenced by individual whose debts are primarily consumer debts		**2002(o)**	Clerk or other designee shall give trustee and all creditors notice by mail of order for relief within 20 days.
	Notices to foreign creditors		**Interim 2002(p)**	If, at the request of a party in interest or the U.S. Trustee, or on its own initiative, the court finds that a notice mailed within the time prescribed by these rules would not be sufficient to give a creditor with a foreign address to which notices under these rules are mailed reasonable notice under the circumstances, the court may order that the notice be supplemented with notice by other means or that the time prescribed for the notice by mail be enlarged. Unless the court for cause orders otherwise, a creditor with a foreign address to which notices under this rule are mailed shall be given at least 30 days notice of the time fixed for filing a proof of claim under Rule 3002(c) or Rule 3003(c).
	Rule 2004 examination		**2004**	On the motion of any party in interest.

DUE DATE	ACTION	CODE §	RULE	EXPLANATION; TIME TO ACT
	Order to compel attendance of debtor for examination		**2005**	On motion of any party in interest supported by an affidavit alleging: (1) that the examination of the debtor is necessary for the proper administration of the estate and that there is reasonable cause to believe that the debtor is about to leave or has left the debtor's residence or principal place of business to avoid examination, or (2) that the debtor has evaded service of a subpoena or of an order to attend for examination, or (3) that the debtor has willfully disobeyed a subpoena or order to attend for examination, duly served, the court may issue to the marshal, or some other officer authorized by law, an order directing the officer to bring the debtor before the court without unnecessary delay. If, after hearing, the court finds the allegations to be true, the court shall thereupon cause the debtor to be examined forthwith. If necessary, the court shall fix conditions for further examination and for the debtor's obedience to all orders made in reference thereto.
	Permissive intervention in case	1109	**2018(a)**	After hearing on such notice as the court directs and for cause shown, the court may permit any interested entity to intervene generally or with respect to any specified matter.
	Computation of time		**9006(a)**	In computing any time prescribed or allowed by the Rules, Fed.R.Civ.P. made applicable by Rules, local rules, court order, or any applicable statute, day of the act, event, or default from which designated period of time begins to run shall not be included; last day of period shall be included unless it is a Saturday, Sunday, or legal holiday, or, when act to be done is filing of paper in court, day on which weather or other conditions made clerk's office inaccessible, in which event period runs until end of the next day which is not one of the above days.
				When period of time prescribed or allowed is less than 8 days, intermediate Saturdays, Sundays, and legal holidays are excluded from computation.
				Legal holidays include New Year's Day, Martin Luther King, Jr.'s Birthday, Washington's Birthday, Memorial Day, Independence Day, Labor Day, Columbus Day, Veterans Day, Thanksgiving Day, Christmas Day, and any other day appointed as a holiday by President, Congress, or state in which court is held.

DUE DATE	ACTION	CODE §	RULE	EXPLANATION; TIME TO ACT
	Enlargement of time		**Interim 9006(b)**	The court, for cause shown, with or without motion or notice, orders relevant period enlarged if the request is made before the expiration of the period originally prescribed or as extended by previous order, or upon motion made after expiration of specified time if failure to act was result of excusable neglect. However, the court may not enlarge time for actions to be taken under Rules 1007(d), 2003(a) and (d), 7052, 9023, and 9024. The court may enlarge time for taking action Rules 1006(b)(2), 1007(c) with respect to the time to file schedules and statements in a small business case, 1017(e), 3002(c), 4003(b), 4004(a), 4007(c), 8002 and 9033, only to the extent and under the conditions stated in those rules.
	Reduction of time		**9006(c)**	The court, for cause shown, with or without motion or notice, may reduce the time to act, except time may not be reduced for actions taken under Rules 2002(a)(7), 2003(a), 3002(c), 3014, 3015, 4001(b)(2), 4001(c)(2), 4003(a), 4004(a), 4007(c), 8002, and 9033(b).
	Time for motions		**9006(d)**	Written motion, and notice of hearing must be served no later than 5 days before time of hearing, unless different time fixed by court or Rules. When motion is supported by affidavit, it must be served with motion; opposing affidavits may be served no later than 1 day prior to hearing.
	Time of service by mail		**9006(e)**	Service of process and service of any paper other than process or of notice by mail is complete on mailing.
	Additional time after service by mail		**9006(f)**	When there is a right or requirement to act or undertake some proceedings within a prescribed period after service and that service is by mail or under Rule 5(b)(2)(C) or (D) Fed.R.Civ.P., 3 days shall be added to the prescribed period.

DUE DATE	ACTION	CODE §	RULE	EXPLANATION; TIME TO ACT
	Contested matters		9014	In contested matter in case under Code not otherwise governed by Rules, relief must be requested by motion, and reasonable notice and opportunity for hearing must be afforded party against whom relief is sought. No response is required unless the court orders an answer to motion.
	Subpoenas		FRCP 45(c) 9016	Person commanded to produce and permit inspection and copying may, within 14 days after service of subpoena or before time specified for compliance if time is less than 14 days, serve written objection; if movant wants to continue, should do so via motion to compel.
	Compromise		9019(a)	On motion and after hearing on notice to creditors, U.S. Trustee, debtor, and indenture trustees as provided in Rule 2002, court may approve compromise or settlement.
	Authority to compromise or settle controversies within classes		9019(b)	After hearing on such notice as court directs, court may fix class or classes of controversies and authorize trustee to compromise or settle controversies within class or classes, without further hearing or notice.
	Contempt other than contempt committed in presence of bankruptcy judge		9020	Rule 9014 governs motion for contempt by the U.S. Trustee or party in interest.
	Entry of judgment		9021 5003	Except as otherwise provided in the Bankruptcy Rules, a judgment is effective when entered as provided in Rule 5003.
	Notice of judgment or order		9022(a)	Immediately upon entry of judgment or order, clerk must give notice of entry by mail on the contesting parties and on other entities as court directs; lack of notice of entry does not affect the time to appeal or relieve or authorize the court to relieve a party for failure to appeal within time allowed, except as permitted in Rule 8002.
	Motion for new trial		9023 FRCP 59(b)	Motion for new trial must be served no later than 10 days after entry of judgment.
			9023 FRCP 59(c)	When motion for new trial is based on affidavits, they must be served with motion; opposing party has 10 days after service to serve opposing affidavits, which may be extended for an additional period not exceeding 20 days.

DUE DATE	ACTION	CODE §	RULE	EXPLANATION; TIME TO ACT
			9023 **FRCP** **59(d)**	No later than 10 days after entry of judgment, and after notice and hearing, court on its own initiative may order new trial.
	Motion to alter or amend judgment		**9023** **FRCP** **59(e)**	Must be served no later than 10 days after entry of judgment.
	Relief from judgment or order (clerical mistakes)		**9024** **FRCP** **60(a)**	May be corrected by court at any time; during pendency of an appeal, such mistakes may be corrected before appeal is docketed in appellate court, and thereafter while appeal is pending may be corrected with leave of appellate court.
	Relief from judgment or order (mistakes, inadvertence, excusable neglect, newly discovered evidence, fraud, etc.)		**9024** **FRCP** **60(b)**	Motion must be made within a reasonable time, and for reasons set forth in FRCP 60(b)(1), (2), and (3), not more than 1 year after judgment, order or proceeding was entered or taken, except: Motion to reopen a case or for reconsideration of an order allowing or disallowing a claim against the estate entered without a contest is not subject to the 1-year limitation period. A complaint to revoke a discharge in a Chapter 7 case may be filed only within time allowed by § 727(e); and A complaint to revoke an order confirming a plan may be filed only within time allowed by §§ 1144 or 1330.

DUE DATE	ACTION	CODE §	RULE	EXPLANATION; TIME TO ACT
	Notice of removal		**9027**	If claim or cause of action in a civil action is pending when a case under the Code is commenced, notice of removal may be filed only within the longest of: (a) 90 days after order for relief, (b) 30 days after entry of an order terminating a stay, if the claim or cause of action has been stayed by § 362, or (c) 30 days after a trustee qualifies in a Chapter 11 case but no later than 180 days after order for relief.
				If bankruptcy case is pending when a claim or cause of action is asserted in another court, notice of removal may only be filed within shorter of: (a) 30 days after receipt, through service or otherwise, of a copy of the initial pleading setting forth the claim or cause of action sought to be removed, or (b) 30 days after receipt of summons if initial pleading is filed with court but not served with the summons.
				Promptly after filing notice of removal, party filing notice must serve copy on all parties to the removed claim or cause of action.
				Promptly after filing notice of removal, party must file copy with clerk of court from which claim or cause of action is removed; removal of the claim or cause of action is effected on filing of copy of notice of removal.
				Any party who has filed a pleading in connection with removed claim, other than party filing notice of removal, must file statement within 10 days after filing of notice admitting or denying core/noncore allegations in notice.
	Defendant's answer in removed action		**9027(g)**	In removed action where defendant has not answered, defendant must answer or present other defenses or objections within 20 days following receipt through service or otherwise of copy of initial pleading setting forth claim for relief on which action or proceeding is based, or within 20 days following service of summons on initial pleading, or within 5 days following filing of notice of removal, whichever is longest.

DUE DATE	ACTION	CODE §	RULE	EXPLANATION; TIME TO ACT
	Review of proposed findings of fact and conclusions of law in noncore proceedings		9033	Bankruptcy judge must file, and clerk must serve, proposed findings of fact and conclusions of law. Within 10 days after being served with a copy, party may serve and file with clerk written objections. Party may respond to another party's objections within 10 days after being served with a copy. Bankruptcy judge may for cause extend time for filing objections for period not to exceed 20 days from expiration of time prescribed; request to extend time must be filed before time for filing objections has expired, except request made no more than 20 days after expiration of time for filing objections may be granted upon showing of excusable neglect.

INDEX

surrender by debtor, 4, 55
swap agreement transfers, 72

T

tax claims, 51–52, 61, 115
tax debt, date of, 73
tax-deferred annuities, 69
tax liability, 48–49, 61, 73, 119
tax refunds, right to, 48
tax returns
    Chapter 11 reorganization plans, requirements, 98, 105, 115
    Chapter 13, requirements, 124, 127
    debtor's duty to provide creditor, 54–55
    expedited review of, 49
    failure to file, 124
    filing of, 24, 56, 57, 124, 127
tenancy evictions, 26–29
time
    computation of, 148
    enlargement of, 149
    for motions, 149
    reduction of, 149
    See also extension of time
transcripts, duty of reporter to prepare and file, 142
transferees, liability of avoided transfer, 77
transfers of claims, 44–45
transfers of property of estate, 71, 73–77
trustee bond, 16
trustees
    Chapter 7, election and duties, 79–82, 83, 87
    Chapter 11, appointment and duties, 94–98, 102, 103, 104, 105, 108, 114
    Chapter 13, appointment and duties, 121–122, 128
    election disputes, 21
    employment of special counsel, 17
    lease obligations, 39, 40
    liability for tax incurred during administration of estate, 49
    as lien creditor, 70
    limitations on avoiding powers of, 71–73
    notice to, 32, 45, 144, 145
    obligation to perform lease obligations, 40
    removal of, 16
    report of creditors entitled to be paid from unclaimed property, 24
    return of goods, 72
    sale or lease of personally identifiable information prohibited, 34
    small business cases, 105
    termination of services upon conversion, 25
    unsecured credit obtainment, 37
Trust Indenture Act (1939), 119

tuition credits or certificates, 69
turnover of property
    conversion to Chapter 7, 83
    by custodian, 70
    to estate, 70
turnover of records, conversion to Chapter 7, 83

U

unclaimed property, 24
undue hardship, 65
United States, actions requiring notices to, 145
unsecured claims
    for domestic support obligations, 50
    filing proof of, 43
    limitation on avoidance of perfected security interests, 73
    priorities of, 50–52
    reduction of, 47
unsecured credit, obtainment, 37–38
unsecured creditors
    additional noncontingent, 15
    avoidance of transfers of interests voidable under law, 70
    Chapter 7, trustee elections, 79
    Chapter 11 reorganization plans, 113, 115
    Chapter 13 plans, objections to, 127
    committee of, 6, 14, 18, 82, 93
    joining involuntary case, 15
    list of, 4, 12, 15
use of property, 33–36, 38, 39
utility companies, 82, 97, 122
utility service, 41–42

V

venue, dismissal and change of, 1
violence, victims of, 86
voluntary cases
    case administration, 11–14
    commencement of, 11
    corporate ownership statements, 11
    dismissal of, 56
    filing fees, 12
    health care business designation, 13
    list of creditors, 2, 11, 12
    list of equity security holders, 11, 12
    petitions, filing and service of, 2
    small business designation, 13

W

wage and salary claims, 51, 114
warehouseman's lien, 72

About the Author

NORMAN L. PERNICK is a partner at Saul Ewing LLP, where he practices in many aspects of bankruptcy and workouts, representing debtors, creditors' committees, secured and unsecured creditors, and trustees. As Chair of the Firm's Bankruptcy and Restructuring Department, Mr. Pernick leads more than 25 attorneys in all aspects of bankruptcy, insolvency and corporate reorganizations. He received his B.A. degree (*magna cum laude* and with high honors in political science) from Brandeis University in 1981 and his J.D. degree (with honors) from The George Washington University in 1984. Mr. Pernick is a member of the Delaware Bar Association and the American Bar Association (Member, Section of Business Law and its Business Bankruptcy Committee).

About the Editor

JAY A. SHULMAN is a partner at Saul Ewing LLP, where he practices in many aspects of bankruptcy and workouts, representing debtors, creditors' committees, secured and unsecured creditors, and trustees. He received his B.A. degree (*magna cum laude,* with distinction in all subjects) from Cornell University, College of Arts and Sciences, in 1973, and his J.D. degree (*cum laude,* Order of the Coif) from Northwestern University in 1977. From 1978–1984, he was engaged in the full-time teaching of bankruptcy and commercial law at the University of Maine and as a visiting associate professor at The George Washington University. Mr. Shulman is a member of the Maryland bar, as well as the American Bar Association (Section of Business Law).